THE KEYS to the Classroom

A basic manual to help new language teachers find their way

BY PAULA PATRICK

Edited by

PAUL PLAWIN

MARTY ABBOTT

STEVE ACKLEY

The American Council on the Teaching of Foreign Languages
1001 North Fairfax Street, Suite 200
Alexandria, VA 22314

Graphic Design by Goulah Design Group, Inc.
Proofreading by Sandy Cutshall, Print Management, Inc.

ISBN: 978-0-9705798-2-9

Foreword

Why didn't anyone ever teach me about this in my methods course? If you're a new teacher, you may have asked yourself that question a dozen times. The answer is probably that there is so much to learn in a methods course that your professors most likely just couldn't fit it all in.

The truth is that surviving your first year(s) of teaching includes all the important things you learned in your teacher preparation program, plus a whole lot more—things you'll learn on the job from colleagues, from your school, and simply from trial and error.

The American Council on the Teaching of Foreign Languages (ACTFL) has produced this handbook to help you avoid, as much as possible, the trials of the errors. In the pages that follow, you will find those exceedingly important tips that help you be as prepared as possible for opening day. You'll find ways of making it through those first challenging weeks when everything is new and you're establishing a sense of comfort and familiarity. And, as those weeks pass, you'll find yourself turning back to this guide as you prepare for Back-to-School Night, parent conferences, grading, and eventually those closing weeks of school. In just a few years, you'll be the one passing on the sage advice you'll find in this handbook, as you become the veteran expert helping to support the novice teachers in your school. But don't give the handbook away! You'll find yourself turning back to it time and again because of all the good ideas that can help a good teacher be a great one.

Teaching is hard work. But then, anything worth doing usually is. The rewards of teaching are endless, and the chance to make a difference in the lives of students, in the future of your local community, and in a global community far exceed the dollars you'll earn. Never forget that good teaching matters, and that the work you do matters more than ever.

All of us, members of ACTFL and veterans in the language teaching profession, are rooting for you. We hope that you meet extraordinary successes, quiet rewards, and students who every day remind you that they are what it's all about.

Good luck!

Myriam Met
National Foreign Language Center
Founding President, NADSFL

To the beginning teachers who shared their fears, frustrations, creative ideas, and solutions; and to my colleagues who are dedicated to providing quality education to America's future.

Introduction

The teaching profession touches so many lives and teachers have such an impact on students that if asked to reflect on one's educational experience, most people would be able to cite a teacher who made a difference for them. Now you have the opportunity to be one of those teachers. As a beginning language teacher, proficient in your subject matter, but not necessarily well-versed in teaching methodology, you will be given a curriculum framework, basic rules and policies, some basic training, and a welcome to the field of teaching. You will also have lots of questions. Don't worry. We have lots of answers for you.

This handbook is designed to get new teachers ready—in short order—to tackle your first teaching assignment. You probably remember some of the savvy techniques your instructors in high school and college used to engage you in the learning process and excite you about learning languages. And we'll review the best of them in the chapters to come. You'll also find lots of tips for setting up your classroom, establishing your grading process, creating an exciting learning environment, and figuring out how to meet your school and district curriculum requirements. We've included many templates you can use as-is or modify and revise as you like. They will save you from reinventing the wheel in the process of establishing yourself as a teacher in your school.

A significant number of teachers—relative rookies as well as wise veterans, plus conference attendees and presenters, specialists, supervisors, and school administrators—contributed to the content of this handbook. You can benefit from their countless hours of classroom teaching, observations, debriefing sessions, teacher workshops, collaboration opportunities, and interventions over many years. We hope this handbook will give you a quick start in getting your classroom teaching career up and running.

Paula Patrick
Foreign Language Coordinator
Fairfax County Public Schools (VA)

Table of Contents

Chapter 1: The First Week

Templates:

Chapter 2: The First Year

Chapter 1 The First Week

Preparing for the first week of school

You have the first day of school circled in red on your calendar. This is a day you have been anticipating, and it is rushing toward you. Are you ready to greet a classroom full of anxious students, waiting for you to guide them in a new learning experience? It is normal to be a bit nervous at this point. But know this: Having read this handbook, you'll know the basic classroom drill. You will have your introductions and explanations down pat. You'll be able to put your students at ease. And before you know it, that first day will be a memory.

The purpose of this handbook is to get you ready in short order to tackle your teaching assignment. You probably remember some of the savvy techniques your instructors in high school and college used to make you excited about learning. We'll review the best of them in the chapters to come. You'll find tips for setting up your classroom, establishing your grading process, creating an effective learning environment, and figuring out how to meet your school and district curriculum requirements. You'll find lots of templates you can use as is or modify and revise as you like. They will save you from re-inventing the wheel in the process of teaching your students a new language.

So let's get started!

Your Letter to Parents

Before you get caught up in the tasks of setting up the classroom, listing student names in your grade book and setting up a bulletin board, take time to write your introductory letter to the parents of your students. It is just as important as the first impression you make at Back-to-School Night. Parents want to know from the start the answers to important questions, such as:

- Is this teacher positive and enthusiastic about teaching?
- Will he or she be fair to my child?
- What are the expectations for my child?
- How can my child be successful in this class?
- How can I help my child be successful?
- How can I keep up with my child's progress?
- What weight will each classroom component have on the final grade?
- How will the final grade be computed?

In your Letter to Parents, answer all these questions in your own words. Keep it brief, but cogent. And when you distribute your letter to students at the end of your first day emphasize that students should present these letters to their parents as soon as they return home.

Before printing out copies of your letter, ask a member of your department to proof it for you. Ask an administrator to review the letter if required to do so by your school district. It's important to make a good first impression with a well-written letter free of any errors. You do not want parents to see any spelling or grammatical errors because they will think: 1) you do not know how to write English correctly, 2) you will be careless in grading their child's work, and 3) you do not take pride in your work.

In your letter, give parents a phone number and an e-mail address where they may contact you at work. An open line of communication gives parents a secure feeling that you share the mission of helping their child succeed. Make your letter as inviting and helpful as possible, and send it home the first day of school. Parents especially look forward to reading the information students bring home after their first day. Have parents sign and return the bottom part of the letter indicating how they prefer to be contacted during the school year.

Note: Parents are sometimes confused when they get letters from five or six different teachers each indicating slightly different procedures. A suggestion here would be to use e-mail as an alternative, especially for middle and high school parents. It's possible to ask the students to request that their parents send you an e-mail indicating how they would prefer to be contacted. If a teacher does not hear from a parent, the teacher knows that a follow up is needed to initiate contact. Teachers can make this the assignment, keep track of the e-mails, create class lists, and send the initial letter electronically. Many schools are restricting paper and encouraging e-mail. Many parents prefer this type of contact since letters do not arrive home. It is important to know if all parents have access to computers. If not, you can tell the parent that you will be sending home information on certain days.

Writing a Syllabus

In some districts, the syllabus for a course is already written. If this is the case in your district, make sure you copy the syllabus and distribute it to your students and parents in accordance to your district policy. If this is not the case, and the expectation is for you to write a syllabus, then ask colleagues for samples of syllabi to read. Even though you may have received numerous syllabi in your courses at college, composing one for students in "your" course may make you nervous initially. Not to worry. A well-written syllabus indicates that you have spent time planning the course and want each student to be prepared for your instruction.

The following items should be included if applicable in your district:

- Course title and course code.
- Credit upon completion.
- Classroom number
- Information on how to get in touch with the instructor.
- Titles of textbook, workbook, supplementary readings.
- Materials needed, such as supplies, dictionaries.
- Course description, with goals and objectives.
- Content to be covered by quarter, semester, or year.
- Policies and/or rules regarding tardies, attendance, cheating, grading, class participation, missed assignments.
- Available sources of support.

Grading System

One of the most difficult changes students face when transitioning from elementary school to middle and high school is having a different teacher, and classroom, for each subject they are enrolled in. In each teacher's class, they may face a new set of rules, different grading system and classroom procedures. To help your students, post your grading policy for all to see at any time. It is also important to include your grading policy in the letter home to parents and in your syllabus. Students and parents alike will appreciate being able to refer to your letter during the year to review your system. The following points will help you to be consistent and clear about how you intend to grade your students' progress:

- Decide from the beginning if you will be using points or percentages. Switching between the two systems is very confusing for students and for parents.
- If you use percentages, decide before school starts if you are going to round up with a .5 or not. Be sure to consult your school or district's policy manual as there may be guidelines for this process.
- Make sure students understand how each marking period will be calculated, along with the final exam, to come up with the final grade for the year.
- Explain to students how much weight each category will have. A percentage on a daily activity and a test will affect the average for the marking period differently.
- Give students a quick example of all the grades that could go into a marking period. Have them make the computations. This exercise will impress upon them the weight of different categories and you will see students putting forth more effort in the areas with more weight.
- If you use a rubric for arriving at performance assessments or projects, give students a copy of it before the assessment or assignment is given. Students should be informed about the criteria for grading before, not after, the project is completed. Remember: students will give you what you ask for. If you did not make your criteria for grading clear, you will not get a quality project in return. Students perform best when they have been given clear expectations and directions and are not left to guess what the teacher wants each student to do.

- Post the school district's policy for what constitutes an A, B, C, D, and F. It may seem clear to you, but some students may have transferred to your school from another district and they may be unfamiliar with the cut-off percentages.

Classroom Rules

I know teachers like to have rules posted for all students to see and often it is a school policy. Keep in mind that the bottom line for classroom management is to make every minute count. When students are engaged in the lesson and not bored, classroom management issues are less likely to occur. If you are required to post your rules or prefer to do so, keep a positive classroom atmosphere. It is easy to write your classroom rules with "Do not _____ or _____ NOT allowed." Rules are much more effective if presented in a positive manner, such as "Be respectful and considerate of others" and "Come prepared to learn." Avoid the word NOT. Limit your list to about five basic rules. A lengthy list is overwhelming and students may feel they can do nothing right.

- List only rules you know you will enforce. If you are inconsistent in enforcing your rules, students will learn quickly that it's not important to follow them.
- Plan your consequences before school starts and not in the middle of an infraction.
- Discuss your rules with your school's administrators and make sure they will support you, before you ever send a student to the office for breaking a rule.
- Some teachers even involve the students in the development of the class rules and therefore have more ownership from the students in the management of the class.
- Students also find it interesting to investigate school or classroom rules in target language schools. This is a great way to involve them in the rule-setting process in an authentic way.

Seating Arrangements

Since communication is a key component of foreign language learning, your seating arrangement should facilitate interaction. Think of ways you can group students and still have the desks conducive to testing. Some teachers arrange their desks in rows because they want to minimize talking at inappropriate times and limit cheating. Straight rows will accomplish this goal, but if you want students to practice with a partner, students will be twisting in their seats while trying to engage their partner. Also, it's easy for students to disengage while talking to the back of their classmates' heads.

Instead of inhibiting productive conversation, rethink how you can keep students on task and involved in the lesson. For example, this can be accomplished by changing activities often and giving students more opportunities to use language in problem-solving. Try changing the seating arrangement each marking period. You can also tell students it is a privilege to sit next to their friends and if they talk at inappropriate times they will lose that seating privilege. Once you have established order in the class, arrange your students' desks in one of the following arrangements:

- Horseshoe: In this arrangement, students are able to see the faces of most of the students in the class and can start conversations easily when asked to do so.
- Tables: In a table formation, you can get groups of 4 to 6 to work together and discuss a topic or break into sub groups. For testing purposes you may want to consider coversheets or science project boards to set up mock cubicles.
- Paired grouping: Students are already paired with a partner. This is ideal for partner drills throughout the lesson.
- Half and half: Have half the class facing the other half. Students are able to look at half the class when asking and answering questions and will also be able to work on partner drills with the person next to them.

The Traveling Teacher

What if you find yourself traveling from room to room, without a permanent base? Before school begins, work out a system with the teachers who also use the classroom. Ask if you can have a bookcase, table, portion of the bulletin board or wall space, drawer of a file cabinet, shelf of a wardrobe, drop boxes, and/or file folder stand.

If this is not possible, you may want to locate a very tall mobile cart. It can become your mobile desk. It will need a place to store handouts, textbooks, workbooks, homework, chalk, whiteboard markers, transparencies and overhead markers, extra paper and pencils, and the like. There are traveling teachers who post their classroom rules to their cart, and students regard the cart as a place to deposit homework, pick up worksheets, and even get a pencil if they have forgotten to bring one. If you have a cart, you'll always have your handouts with you.

Bulletin Boards/Classroom Décor

There are two camps when it comes to bulletin boards: teachers that love decorating them and those who lack the creative confidence to design a unique bulletin board that will also function as an additional instructional resource for students. If you love designing and changing a bulletin board display often, you can probably skip this section, because you will find a way to squeeze in the time to do so. For those of you who find yourself staring at a rather large bulletin board in your classroom and wondering what on earth you can do with it, here are some suggestions:

- Ask a teacher who enjoys creating bulletin boards for ideas.
- Display material by marking period, semester, or entire year.
- Address thematic units in more than one level and/or language (if you have more than one preparation). You could list all the themes you will cover for that year by level and/or language (especially if you teach more than one level or language).
- Post items that catch students' attention and are informative.
- Post student work. This is a great way to make use of bulletin board space while featuring the creative work of your students.
- Make your board a low maintenance tool.

Bulletin board content ideas:

- Create a collage of everyday material such as food and drink labels, advertisements, coasters, candy wrappers, empty food containers, CD covers, newspaper headlines, magazine covers, and souvenirs brought in by students as evidence of products made or consumed in a particular country, plus notices of current events and foreign cultural information. You could build a bulletin board you would never have to change for the entire year.
- Build a bulletin board of classroom commands/expressions with pictures attached. This will remind all students to stay in the target language no matter what the level of instruction that is being taught. They will take risks and start using the expressions in their writings. Put sentences, commands and questions on the bulletin board in the target language—such as "Open your book to page 57." "I forgot my pencil." "The early bird gets the worm." "I can do this!" Then even level 1 students will be able to practice using the target language instead of reverting back to English.
- Develop a timeline for the year on the bulletin board, showing students where they are going at a particular level and let them mark their progress as they go. Teachers can draw lines from the timeline to samples of student work along the way. Be careful not to show a student's name along with a grade if you post student samples, because student grades are always private information.
- Create a bulletin board of pictures from countries that speak the target language. Some of the best pictures can be found in large wall calendars. Take the calendar apart, cut out the pictures, laminate them and staple them onto your bulletin board. Note: Teachers need to pay attention to copyright laws when using copyrighted materials.
- Turn the bulletin board into a smorgasbord of newspaper articles in the target language. Every Friday ask five students to bring in an article in the target language from newspaper websites you have approved. Have them present it briefly for a minute or two, then post the article on the bulletin board. In lower level classes, students can find cognates and guess what the article is saying. If you do not have upper-level students, then perhaps the language honor society students can bring articles by the classroom for service credit. At the end of the year, not only will students find they can understand more than they did at the beginning of the year, but they can also look over the world events that took place that school year.

Equipment

Before the first day of school, check the equipment that is in your classroom(s). Make sure the overhead projector has a working light bulb, the VCR and/or DVD player work, the maps pull down, the markers for the white boards have ink, and you have enough transparencies and overhead markers. Check your computer, LCD projector, CD/cassette recorder, and if you have a Smartboard, make sure you know how it works. There is nothing worse than to start a class session and find out that your equipment doesn't work. Make a list of people you need to contact (when and where) for repairs and supplies. High- and low-tech breakdowns make for disrupted teaching days.

Technology

Technology can be your friend or, at times, your worst enemy. Well ahead of opening day, ask at your school what technology you will have access to for finalizing grades, contacting parents, accessing student information, posting homework on websites, creating lessons, filing lessons, researching facts, using programs that enhance instruction, assessing students, and so forth.

This is extremely important advice. Once school starts, it is hard to find time to learn about and practice with the technology available at your school. Around the mid-year point, you will hear the horror stories about new teachers who have only then discovered that their lives could have been so much easier if they had known about this or that piece of technology. For example, late in the year one teacher finally discovered she could e-mail grades right from her school's grading program to parents' e-mail accounts on a regular basis. To her chagrin, she had been sending grades one by one to parents who wanted updates. Fortunately, a colleague told her there was an easier way.

Find out early if your school's teachers have access to a course management system, like Blackboard.com. Ask if you can get help in developing a website where you can post homework assignments and e-mail homework to students who are sick. Find out if there are free sites for teachers to use where teachers can post homework for parents and students to check on a daily basis.

There are also helpful websites where teachers can get tips and teaching freebies, such as clip art, puzzles, and games. There is a wealth of information on teacher websites. Run searches on your PC to see what resources are available. Bookmark sites that are most beneficial. Also bookmark websites of other local, regional, and national professional organizations that can assist you in your career. The benefits of becoming a member of professional organizations will be discussed later in this handbook.

Emergency Lesson Plans

Admit it—teachers are not super heroes, even if their deeds entitle them to that status. You can get sick. Your car can break down on the way to work. Unanticipated events that will keep you out of your classroom happen. So you need to plan for them. Before the school year begins, develop a lesson plan that can cover three days and is not tied to any particular unit. This may sound challenging, but it really isn't all that difficult and it will save you from having to write lesson plans at 2:00 a.m. because you can't be at school that day. The objective is to allow students to continue to learn in the teacher's absence. Don't design an emergency lesson plan just to keep the students busy, make sure there is an important instructional objective. Make your plan meaningful and easy for a substitute teacher to deliver. If you teach two or more levels, try to develop emergency lesson plans that can be used in all of your classes. The following are suggestions for lessons that can cover up to three days and also be taught by a non-speaker of the language you teach, as many foreign language teachers will not always have access to substitutes who speak the target language.

- Geography lesson: Students can always benefit from a short lesson or refresher lesson on geography and map reading in the country of the target language. Students can also investigate a particular city or region.
- Culture lesson: Upper-level students can create cultural activities for lower-level students, and lower-level students can investigate and write what they have learned on particular cultural topics.
- Children's book: Students may enjoy writing a children's book in the target language, with illustrations. Even level 1 students can write a short story with greetings, numbers, common phrases, and the like. They may be impressed that they can actually produce something in a foreign language and read it aloud to a small group. The illustrations will add some fun to the project. If the substitute can get access to a computer lab, the students may be able to use pictures and creative fonts to give their book a polished look.
- Puppet show: Students can create simple puppets and in small groups write a script for a puppet show. Students learn a great deal from peer editing. For a level 1 class, the teacher may want to provide sample phrases from which the students can select what they need. The teacher may want to pre-record phrases in the script on tape so the class can practice pronunciations.
- Famous people project: Have biographies on 10 or 15 well-known people from the target language country. Ask each student to select a person and read about him or her, then write an essay as if he or she were that person and present it verbally to the class in the target language. In a lower-level class where the students may not able to do this, an alternative would be to ask the students to research their subject person and present profiles of them in English.
- Video: Have a video approved and ready to show to your classes. Make sure it is age appropriate and can be linked to instruction. Develop worksheets for a pre-lesson (containing vocabulary and general information that is useful for the video) as well as post-video worksheets that will provoke discussion. It is also a good idea to have students write a reflection paragraph or essay so that they can digest what they have just viewed and link it to the language, culture, and unit that has just been taught or will be taught.

- Textbook challenge: Don't assume students know where to find information in their textbooks concerning vocabulary, rules, usage, and the like. They have to be taught where how and where to find specific information in their primary resource—the textbook. So create a "Textbook Challenge" activity, with rewards, for students to do while you are away. This can be done at any level as long as the students use a textbook as a resource. For example, ask students to find certain vocabulary words, identify which chapter they are introduced in, if the word has two or more meanings, how the word is used in a sentence, and so forth.

Or have students find grammar points from the index and write down the page numbers where they can be found. Also ask students to locate cultural topics in the table of contents and to describe how a chapter is set up—how the theme is divided, how vocabulary is introduced, how the grammar is introduced, and whether there are partner drills and writing drills. This activity will teach students how to use the textbook as a resource throughout the year and beyond. Substitutes can also participate in this exercise and help students with the questions.

Colleagues: A Valuable Resource

Before school starts, take the time to get to know colleagues, especially experienced teachers, who teach the same or similar courses that you are about to teach. You'll find that they usually will be happy to share information that that you may find crucial for planning and pacing your first month on the job. Ask questions that will help you with immediate issues. Avoid being drawn into long conversations about issues that do not concern you or your course. To stay on topic, have your questions written down. Ask for specific information you'll need to create your syllabus, your letter to parents, and your lessons for the first weeks. Some suggested questions:

- Are there departmental policies on grading, class participation, homework, cheating, classroom rules that I need to know about so I can develop my policies?
- Did you integrate last year's material (level 2 class or above) throughout your lessons this year?
- How many grades do you average a week and per marking period?
- What type of assessments do you use?
- What materials do you use to supplement the textbook?
- Where can I find a copy of the curriculum guide?
- How much material are you able to cover in the first marking period?
- Does the department use common assessments, performance assessments, or departmental exams? Could I get copies before I start planning?
- Do we have common planning time?
- Does the department share materials? Are they located in a central location?
- Do we have access to computers or a computer lab? Do we have to sign up for time?

Student Names

One of your major challenges the first month of school is learning approximately 150 student names and faces. Finding a method that works for you requires some experimentation. Some foreign language teachers ask students to pick a name common to the target language—but this can create more stress during the first month of school because the names have now doubled to 300! Here are some methods experienced teachers use:

- On your seating chart, place students in alphabetical order by first name instead of last name. Proponents of this method say it is easier to remember the first name this way.
- Ask students what their favorite activity is and then group them by activity. If you have students with the same name, this helps you identify which one you are looking for. Also, you probably will remember what a student's favorite activity grouping is. This can be helpful when you want to inquire about their interests. Your students will be impressed that you remember what they like to do.
- Have students decorate table tent cards bearing their names and keep them in place for at least the first month. Let students decorate their tent cards in ways that demonstrate their special interests. That can also elicit dialogue in class.
- Place your seating chart where you can see it, but it is not visible to students.
- Play a name game as a warm-up at the start of each class period for the first week of school.

First Week's Lessons

The first week is always interesting. Teachers who develop lessons for the full class period find they sometimes run out of time. Be sure you know what all of your responsibilities will be in your first week before writing lesson plans for that week. In the first few days of school, many schools have teachers distribute and collect important documents and go over fire drill information, student responsibilities and rights, supplies needed, the course syllabus, and classroom rules. Be prepared for contingencies and interruptions this week. This is a good time for review and use of the target language to get to know your students. Following are suggested activities for the first week:

Level 1

- Alphabet, phonetics, tones, character strokes
- Greetings and introductions
- Names common to the target language
- Cognates, if applicable
- Culture

Level 2

- Student introductions
- Student discussions on family, leisure time activities, likes and dislikes
- "All about me" posters (each student makes a poster describing key physical and social characteristics)
- Review of themes and topics from level 1 integrated in activities as a review, while teaching new material

Level 3

- Review of level 2 themes and topics
- Detailed student introductions
- Discussion of summer activities or travel
- Discussion on current events
- Movie and/or book critiques
- Describing pictures (to get students to use adjectives)

Upper Level

- Activities involving assigned summer reading
- Discussion on current events
- Movie and/or book critiques
- Discussion and reflection regarding student responsibilities and suggestions for changes in school policies
- Comparison of environmental policies between U.S. and target language country

Dress for Success

Many young teachers may be inclined to identify with the students they teach. After all, they are relatively close in age to students, especially those in upper-level classes. You must keep in mind, however, that you are a professional in charge of many students in a classroom. You must firmly establish that role in every way. And your work attire is a major factor in defining roles of teachers and students. If you come to work in casual clothing, such as jeans and a t-shirt, you are sure to look like most of your students, and it will be hard for students to regard you as an authority figure.

Some school districts have a dress policy for teachers, but if there is no policy, you must think carefully about what your physical appearance is telling students in the class. The message should be, "I am in charge." If your school has a "dress down Friday," ask more experienced teachers for dress code tips before showing up in shorts and a tank top. Here are a couple of tips for dressing for success:

- Definitely dress your best for parent conferences, Back-to-School Night, and award presentations. This sends a message to parents that the teacher is a professional and expects to be treated as one.
- Wear slacks, tucked-in shirts, skirts and/or dresses, appropriate shoes, and socks or stockings. (Ties for men are required in some schools). It is best to ask your administrator.
- Definitely avoid beach wear, including flip flops, short skirts, tank tops showing underwear, midriff, cleavage, jeans with holes and tears, and see-through clothing.
- Some schools have spirit days to support an activity or sporting event. Ask veteran teachers what is allowed by the administration before coming to school in inappropriate attire.
- Holiday attire and/or costumes may be permitted by some school districts, but banned by others, especially if the clothing has religious overtones. It is always best to ask first.

Am I Ready?

☐ I have prepared my **letter to parents.**

- ☐ I have asked a member of my department to proof the letter/email.
- ☐ The letter/e-mail has been approved by the appropriate administrator.

☐ I have copied the district's syllabus or

☐ I have prepared a **course syllabus** that includes:

- ☐ Course title and course code.
- ☐ Credit upon completion.
- ☐ Classroom number
- ☐ Information on how to get in touch with the instructor.
- ☐ Titles of textbook, workbook, and supplementary readings.
- ☐ Materials needed, such as supplies and dictionaries.
- ☐ Course description, with goals and objectives.
- ☐ Content to be covered by quarter, semester, or year.
- ☐ Policies and/or rules regarding tardies, attendance, cheating, grading, class participation, and missed assignments.
- ☐ Available sources of support.

☐ I have explained the following points of my **grading policy** to parents and students in writing:

- ☐ I have explained that I calculate points/percentages for each grade.
- ☐ I have clearly stated that I will/will not round up grades.
- ☐ I have explained how each marking period and final year grade will be calculated.
- ☐ I have explained how much weight each category will have.
- ☐ I have included a copy of the rubric(s) I use for assessing student work.
- ☐ I have included the school district's policy for what constitutes: A, B, C, D, & F.

☐ I have developed my essential **classroom rules.**

- ☐ I have developed positive rules and limited the number of rules to only those that are essential.

☐ I have well-developed lessons that will keep my students engaged the entire period.

☐ I have paced my lessons appropriately and have a back-up plan for any remaining time in a period, in order to limit classroom management issues.

☐ I have developed a **seating arrangement** that will encourage communication and collaboration.

☐ Since I am **not in one classroom** for all my classes, I have developed a system to help me stay organized while I travel.

- ☐ I have worked out a system with the teacher who also uses the classroom.
- ☐ I have a bookcase, table, section of the bulletin board or wall space, drawer of a file cabinet, shelf of a wardrobe, drop boxes and/or file folder stand to store my materials.
- ☐ I have a traveling cart with room for all my materials for each class.

☐ I have decorated my **bulletin board(s)** so that students will feel welcomed and enthusiastic about learning the target language.

☐ I have checked all **equipment** to make sure everything is operational, and I know how to operate each piece of equipment.

☐ I have registered for **technology** training so that I am current on the technology required/recommended for my teaching position.

☐ I have developed three days of **emergency lesson plans**.
- ☐ My lessons can either be used for any class or are marked for the specific level.
- ☐ My lessons are written so that a substitute can follow them, even if he or she does not speak the language.
- ☐ I have provided materials and copies of handouts for the lessons and they are marked appropriately.
- ☐ My lessons allow students to continue to learn in my absence.

☐ I have collaborated with colleagues and feel I have my immediate questions answered.

☐ I have developed a system for being able to call students by name, even on the first day.

☐ I have planned the first week's lessons so that students feel they are learning something new and exciting from the first day on.

☐ I have selected clothing that is appropriate for my professional position.

Reflection

What aspect of starting the school year worked well?

What would I change for next year?

How would I change it?

What additional resources do I need to gather for next year?

Template A Sample Letter to Parents (modern language)

Mountain View High School *Home of the Mountain View Tigers*

5345 Tiger Trail [date]
Pleasant Town, USA

I am pleased to have your son/daughter in my German 1 class. I plan to make his/her year of studying a foreign language an exciting and memorable experience.

Foreign language study is essential today not only to meet the requirements of higher education institutions, but also because of the expanding global economy and ever increasing job opportunities requiring one or more languages other than English. Rapid expansion of international business creates a need for more knowledge of international cultures as well as proficiency in foreign languages. In order to prepare our future leaders to be competitive, students must develop communicative competence in languages.

Emphasis will be placed on communicating effectively in German, making connections, comparing German with the English language, examining communities, and understanding the cultures of the German-speaking countries. At the beginning of each marking period, I will send home objectives for the nine weeks. If you have any questions about the program, please feel free to contact me at [phone number] or e-mail me at faye.fantastic@mountainview.edu.

In order to strengthen your child's organizational skills, I will be issuing each student a Mountain View Planner, in which he or she is to write assignments and quizzes/tests/projects at the beginning of each week. Please check your child's planner regularly to be informed of the daily activities. Homework assignments will be kept to an average of 15-20 minutes per day. Each student will be responsible for maintaining a log of his or her grades. I will issue each student an interim report. This computer printout of all grades to date can be requested at any time as a progress report.

Student grades are based on a point system. Each grade the student receives (quiz, test, oral presentation, project, class participation, etc.) will be worth a certain number of points based on a 100-point scale. Quarter and final grades will be based on the school district's grading scale which is as follows:

94 - 100	A
87 - 93	B
80 - 86	C
70 - 79	D
Below 70	F

At the end of the marking period, the total number of points earned will be divided by the total number of points possible. Each grade has the following weight for the quarter grade:

Tests	30%
Quizzes	20%
Projects	25%
Homework	15%
Class Participation	10%

Students do not receive grades lower than 50% unless the student refuses to complete the assignment or is caught cheating. The final grade for the year is an average of the four quarter grades and the final exam.

I expect this to be an exciting and fulfilling year in your child's foreign language experience and I am looking forward to meeting you at Back-to-School Night on [date].

Sincerely,

Faye Fantastic
German Instructor

Template B | Sample Letter to Parents (Latin)

Mountain View High School *Home of the Mountain View Tigers*

5345 Tiger Trail [date]

Pleasant Town, USA

Dear Parents,

I am pleased to have your son/daughter in my Latin 1 class. I plan to make his/her year of studying a foreign language an exciting and memorable experience.

Foreign language study is essential today not only to meet the requirements of higher education institutions, but also because of the expanding global economy and ever increasing job opportunities domestically requiring one or more languages other than English. Students will benefit from learning **Latin** no matter what academic or career path they pursue.

The relationship of English to **Latin** is emphasized in vocabulary building, word derivation, and meanings of prefixes and suffixes. Language structures and syntax are developed through the study of literary passages. At the beginning of each marking period, I will send home objectives for the nine weeks. If you have any questions about the program, please feel free to contact me at [phone number] or e-mail me at faye.fantastic@mountainview.edu.

In order to strengthen your child's organizational skills, I will be issuing each student a Mountain View Planner, in which he or she is to write assignments and quizzes/tests/projects at the beginning of each week. Please check your child's planner regularly to be informed of the daily activities. Homework assignments will be kept to an average of 15-20 minutes per day. Each student will be responsible for maintaining a log of his or her grades. I will issue each student an interim report. This computer printout of all grades to date can be requested at any time as a progress report.

Student grades are based on a point system. Each grade the student receives (quiz, test, oral presentation, project, class participation, etc.) will be worth a certain number of points based on a 100-point scale. Quarter and final grades will be based on the school district's grading scale which is as follows:

94 - 100	A
87 - 93	B
80 - 86	C
70 - 79	D
Below 70	F

At the end of the marking period, the total number of points earned will be divided by the total number of points possible. Each grade has the following weight for the quarter grade:

Tests	30%
Quizzes	20%
Projects	25%
Homework	15%
Class Participation	10%

Students do not receive grades lower than 50% unless the student refuses to complete the assignment or is caught cheating. The final grade for the year is an average of the four quarter grades and the final exam.

I expect this to be an exciting and fulfilling year in your child's foreign language experience and I am looking forward to meeting you at Back-to-School Night on [date].

Sincerely,

Faye Fantastic

Template C | Sample Letter to New Student in Class

High School

Mountain View High School — *Home of the Mountain View Tigers*

5345 Tiger Trail — [date]

Pleasant Town, USA

Dear Steven,

It is so nice having you in my French 1 class! I know it is hard joining a class after the start of school because you have missed the teachers' introductions to the courses and their policies and rules. In order to make things a little easier for you, I have outlined my policies and procedures in this letter. Please feel free to ask me questions anytime—my door is always open.

- **Grading:** Student grades are based on a point system. Each grade the student receives (quiz, test, oral presentation, project, class participation, etc.) will be worth a certain number of points as determined by the teacher. At the end of the marking period, the total number of points earned will be divided by the total number of points possible. Each grade has the following weight for the quarter grade:

Tests	30%
Quizzes	20%
Projects	25%
Homework	15%
Class Participation	10%

Students do not receive grades lower than 50% unless the student refuses to complete the assignment or is caught cheating. The final grade for the year is an average of the four quarter grades and the final exam.

- **Class Participation:** Class participation in the target language is a key component in practicing your communicative skills, which are essential in language proficiency. Participation involves more than just raising your hand. Students have to be attentive, participate in partner activities, speak the target language formally and informally, and come to class prepared. If your teacher agrees that you exceed expectations in this area, you will be able to drop your lowest quiz grade at the end of the quarter. These self-assessments will be conducted weekly in order to keep you focused on your progress in this area.

- **Materials:** You will need to come to class each day with a three-ring binder and five dividers. Label each divider 1) Vocabulary Activities, 2) Journal, 3) Reading Selections, 4) Listening Activities, 5) Homework. Please have a calendar/assignment book, pen or pencil, and plenty of paper with you daily.

- **Homework:** It is necessary to practice **French** daily in order to build a solid foundation for future lessons. In order to accomplish this objective, homework will be assigned at the end of each class period. I will post the weekly assignments, quizzes and tests on the board in front of the class, and on my website. It will be your responsibility to record the assignments in your assignment book. If you have been absent, you will know the assignment that has been missed.

- **Extra help:** I am available after school on Mondays and Wednesdays in my room. Please schedule to stay after school with me if you feel you need extra help. It is better to ask for extra help as soon as there is confusion. We also have honor society students willing to help tutor, if you prefer a peer tutor.

Sincerely,

Mme Merveilleuse

Template D | Sample Syllabus

Syllabus for Arabic 1

Course code: 501000
Prerequisite: None
Textbook: *Iqra.* International Educational Foundation. 2003.

Materials needed: Students will need to bring to class a three-ring binder, pen and/or pencil, highlighter, dictionary, and journal.

Course Description
Students develop the ability to communicate about themselves and their immediate environment using simple sentences containing basic language structures. This communication is evidenced in all four language skills—listening, speaking, reading and writing—with emphasis on the ability to communicate orally and in writing. Students begin to explore and study the themes of Personal and Family Life, School Life, Social Life, and Community Life.

Goals: This course's primary goals are to:

- **Communicate in Arabic**
  Students function in a variety of practical settings using listening, speaking, reading, and writing skills as well as knowledge of the target culture(s).
- **Understand other cultures**
  Students demonstrate an understanding of traditions, customs, beliefs, and cultural contributions and how these elements relate to language.
- **Connect with other disciplines and acquire information**
  Students connect information about the language and cultures they are learning with concepts studied in other subject areas.
- **Develop insight into their own language and culture**
  Through study of language and culture, students recognize, compare, and contrast language concepts as well as cultural perspectives, practices, and products.
- **Participate in the global community**
  Students use the foreign language to communicate with speakers of that language, both at home and around the world, to improve their own communication skills and to enhance their view of themselves as citizens of the world.

Content to be covered in the first quarter:
Introductory Unit:
Alphabet & Phonetics
Classroom Expressions

Theme: Personal and Family Life
Greeting and Introductions
Physical Descriptions
Family Members

Assessments: Students will be assessed formally and informally through a variety of means to include quizzes, tests, and projects. These assessments will measure language learning in speaking, writing, listening, and reading. The district has developed and uses the performance assessment as a tool to measure language progress. Performance assessments are conducted routinely throughout the year and are rated using rubrics developed by foreign language teachers. The end-of-year performance assessment counts as 50% of the final exam grade.

Tardies: After two tardies, I will notify parents and assign the student an after-school detention.

Homework: It is necessary to practice Arabic daily in order to build a solid foundation for future lessons. In order to accomplish this objective, homework will be assigned at the end of each class period. I will post the weekly assignments, quizzes, and tests on the board in front of the class, and on my website. It will be your responsibility to record the assignments in your assignment book. If you have been absent, you will know the assignment that has been missed.

Class Participation: Class participation in the target language is a key component in practicing your communicative skills, which are essential in language proficiency. Participation involves more than just raising your hand. Students have to be attentive, participate in partner activities, speak the target language formally and informally, and come to class prepared. If your teacher agrees that you exceed expectations in this area, you will be able to drop your lowest quiz grade at the end of the quarter. These self-assessments will be conducted weekly in order to keep you focused on your progress in this area.

Grading: Student grades are based on a point system. Each grade the student receives (quiz, test, oral presentation, project, class participation, etc,) will be worth a certain number of points as determined by the teacher. At the end of the marking period, the total number of points earned will be divided by the total number of points possible. Each grade has the following weight for the quarter grade.

Tests	30%
Quizzes	20%
Projects	25%
Homework	15%
Class Participation	10%

Extra help: I am available after school on Mondays and Wednesdays in my room. Please schedule to stay after school with me if you feel you need extra help. It is better to ask for extra help as soon as there is confusion. We also have honor society students willing to help tutor, if you prefer a peer tutor.

Template E | Classroom Rules

Classroom Rules and Procedures

Sensational Sensei
Japanese 1

1

Respect your fellow classmates, your teacher, and the contents of the classroom at all times.

2

Come prepared to learn by bringing your textbook, workbook, notebook, and pen/pencil.

3

Food and gum interfere with oral communication.
Please leave these items in your backpack or locker.

4

Ask for clarification the minute you are confused.
There are no dumb questions.

5

Communication is the focus of this class, but not on cell phones.
Leave them in your locker/at home.

Template F | Student Responsibility

What Is Student Responsibility?

1. The state, quality, or fact of being responsible.
2. Something for which one is responsible; a duty, obligation, or burden.

http://dictionary.reference.com/search?q=responsibility

What Is Cheating?

I. The following constitutes cheating in my class:
   a. Giving or receiving information on assessments.
   b. Using any type of unapproved aide during formal or informal assessments (electronic devices, cheat sheets, etc).
   c. Copying software.
   d. Copying information from another student's tests, quizzes, homework, and projects.
   e. Discussing content material with students who have not yet taken an assessment.
   f. Parental help beyond that of assistance.
   g. Talking during an assessment.
   h. Plagiarism: Copying the essential character of another's work, whether visual or written, and submitting it as your own.

II. Consequences for your actions:
   a. I will have a conversation with your parent or guardian.
   b. Your administrator and guidance counselor will be notified.
   c. You will not receive credit for the work that was compromised.
   d. You will have to work hard to earn my trust again.

I will gladly write letters of recommendation for any student who has resisted the temptation to cheat.

Template G | Class Participation

High School

Class Participation Self-Assessment

Class participation is a key component in practicing your communicative skills, which are essential in language proficiency. Participation involves more than just raising your hand. Students have to be attentive, participate in partner activities, speak the target language formally and informally, and come to class prepared. If your teacher agrees that you exceed expectations in this area, you will be able to drop your lowest quiz grade at the end of the quarter. These weekly self-assessments will keep you focused on your progress in this area.

Name: ______________________________ Period ____________

Date: ______________ Language: _______________________

Place a check in the box indicating your participation in these activities over the past week:

1 = occasionally, 2 = half the time, 3 = most of the time, 4 = always

Activity	1	2	3	4
I brought my textbook, notebook, and writing materials to class.				
I paid attention in class and conversed only when asked to do so.				
I raised my hand to answer questions.				
I participated in partner drills.				
I participated in other activities when asked to do so.				
I spoke the target language when spoken to.				
I spoke the target language informally in class.				
I came to class with my homework completed and was able to participate when my teacher went over the assignment.				
Student's Self-Assessment Total Score: ______/32				
Teacher's Validation Score: ______/32				

Conversion Chart:

Exceeds Expectations		Meets Expectations		Almost Meets Expectations	
32	100%	25	92%	17	83%
31	99%	24	91%	16	82%
30	98%	23	89.5%	15	80.5%
29	96%	22	88.5%	14	79.5%
28	95%	20	86%	13	78%
27	94%	19	85%	12	77%
26	93%	18	84%	11	76%

Template H | Emergency Lesson Plan 1

Emergency Lesson Plan: Level 1

All the materials for this lesson are in this manila envelope. Please do not worry if you do not speak German. I have provided a list of expressions in German and English for you to use.

High School German 1
Theme: Social Life
Topic: Weather and Seasons
Targeted standards: ______________________________

Objective:
- Students will ask and answer questions about the weather and seasons.

Essential learning:
- Students will express months and numbers associated with weather and seasons.
- Students will ask and answer questions about the weather.
- Students will identify seasons and the weather associated with each.

How this lesson connects with what has already been learned:
- Students have learned weather expressions. Producing weather posters will review weather expressions. Ask students to identify words they recognize and to guess what season it is.
- The graphic organizer will have students produce words and phrases on their own related to weather expressions and seasons.

How to engage the student:
- Tell students that today they will be able to ask and answer questions about the weather.
- Present pictures of several weather conditions and review the weather expressions that have been previously learned.
- Have students share their own opinion of today's weather. (*It is warm. The sun is shining. It is not windy.*)

Today's lesson:

- Ask students to follow your model on the overhead transparency or board and write out weather expressions for each season on the four index cards you provided.
- Have students turn to a student sitting close to them for five minutes to ask what the weather is like in a particular season (*What is the weather like in the winter?*). Students respond using their index card as a cue if needed (*The weather is cold*). Students record what their partner says on the back of their index card (e.g., *In the winter the weather is cold. It is hot in the summer.*).
- On the overhead transparency showing pictures of various weather scenes, have students come up and write a weather expression under the picture. Have them guess what season is by asking a student: *When is it hot?*
- Ask students to clarify their findings by responding to a few follow-up questions.
- Hand each student a piece of construction paper and have him or her divide the paper in fourths. Have students label each quarter panel with the name of a season. Students then are to draw a weather scene for each season and write as many expressions as possible under each scene.

Student reflection:

- Have students consult the overhead transparency or board for any weather expression they forgot to include.
- Have students think about weather conditions in other parts of the world.

How this lesson affects the next lesson:

Explain that tomorrow they will learn how to deliver a weather report. In a few days, they will present a weather report and a forecast to the class using weather maps.

Materials included in this packet:

Weather posters
Overhead transparencies of weather scenes or pictures to be posted on the board
Construction paper
Index cards
A list of weather expressions in English and in the target language for substitute teacher

Template I

Emergency Lesson Plan 2

Emergency Lesson Plan: Level 3

All the materials for this lesson are in this manila envelope. Please do not worry if you do not speak the target language. The students will be able to work collaboratively in groups.

High School Spanish 3
Theme: Environment
Topic: Ecology
Targeted standards: ______________________________

Objective:
- Students will ask and answer questions about ecology.

Essential learning:
- Students will understand and produce vocabulary related to ecological issues.
- Students will ask and answer questions related to conservation.
- Students will incorporate the conditional mood into their communication using clauses with "should."

How this lesson connects with what has already been learned:
- Students have created posters on ecology prior to this lesson. The posters are posted on the wall. The students may use the posters to generate ideas. Students will utilize the learned vocabulary when producing a children's book on ecology.
- Students will use a graphic organizer to capture learned words and phrases related to ecological issues and conservation.

How to engage the student:
- Tell students that today they will start writing a 20-page children's book on ecology and conservation. They will be able to ask and answer questions about the ecology and conservation.
- Have students share ideas about how one should present information to 6-year-old children.

Today's lesson:

- Ask students to form groups of four and distribute the handouts which include instructions.
- Each student will have an assignment: 1) recorder, 2) editor, 3) illustrator, 4) publisher.
- Have students brainstorm how they want to present the information to children.
- Ask students to clarify their findings by responding to a few questions provided in the handout.
- Hand each group a packet of 20 sheets of blank paper and ask them to create a draft of the questions/answers that will go on each page.
- The students will have the following responsibilities:
- The **recorder** will write down the ideas for each page.
- The **illustrator** will suggest pictures/images that should be included.
- The **editor** will edit the language structures, content, and vocabulary.
- The **publisher** will arrange the content and decide on the layout of the book.

Reflection:

- Have students consult their textbooks (and authentic material provided in this packet) for any ecology/conservation expressions they forgot to include.
- Have students think about ecological issues in Spanish-speaking countries.

How this lesson affects the next lesson:

Explain that the next lesson will be devoted to completing the book and peer editing. When the project is finished, the students will send the books to the neighboring elementary school that has a large Spanish-speaking population for display in its library.

Materials included in this packet:

Posters with vocabulary related to ecology and conservation
Instruction packets for each student
Authentic articles on ecology (that have already been discussed)
Packets of 20 blank sheets (one per group)
Rubric on how the project will be assessed

Chapter 2 The First Year

Prepare to Make the First Year the Best

So you made it through the first week and students are settling down. Routines are established. Things couldn't be better. You may even sense a bit of euphoria. Don't give in to it. There is a lot more you need to prepare for—such as Back-to-School Night, the parent who wants a conference with you as soon as possible, and setting up your goals for the year. Put that would-be euphoria on check. Now is the time to think about goals, assessments, communicating with parents, and other tasks. Look ahead to stay ahead and avoid bumps in the road. This chapter will focus on maintaining a routine and preparing for issues a teacher may face in the first year.

Successful Planning and Goal-Setting

Standards-based education has been growing since the 1990s and has shaped the way teachers write goals, develop lessons, and evaluate student performance. Standards-based education requires teachers to identify what students will be able to do and what they should know at the end of the lesson or unit. Thus you must keep course goals and objectives firmly in focus as you develop lesson plans and assessments.

The course objectives may be determined by your district curriculum. If this is the case, please refer to your curriculum guide when planning. If you are asked to develop **long-term and short-term course goals** and objectives, you should make sure they are aligned with your state standards. For example, Fairfax County, Virginia Public Schools uses the following goals for the Spanish Level 2 course. They are aligned with both the State Standards of Learning and the National Foreign Language Standards.

At the end of **Level 2 Spanish**, students will be able to:

Communicate in Spanish

- Students function in a variety of practical settings using listening, speaking, reading, and writing skills as well as knowledge of the target culture(s).

Understand other cultures

- Students demonstrate an understanding of traditions, customs, beliefs, and cultural contributions and how these elements relate to language.

Connect with other disciplines and acquire information

- Students connect information about the language and cultures they are learning with concepts studied in other subject areas.

Develop insight into their own language and culture

- Through study of language and culture, students recognize, compare, and contrast language concepts as well as cultural perspectives, practices, and products.

Participate in the global community

- Students use the foreign language to communicate with speakers of that language, both at home and around the world, to improve their own communication skills and to enhance their view of themselves as citizens of the world.

When you develop course goals for a **marking period,** take into account the "themes" and "topics" you will cover during that period of time. Use the same process to indicate what students should be able to do in each of the "standards" relative to the topics taught. For example, Fairfax County Public Schools teachers of Spanish have written the following "goals" for the theme

Personal and Family Life, Topic: *Greetings and Introductions,* which is taught during the first month of **Level 1 Spanish:**

Communication

"Person-to-Person Communication"

- Use appropriate forms of address to children, peers, and adults when making introductions.
- Use appropriate gestures and expressions of greeting and leave-taking.
- Ask and respond to simple questions about someone else's identity and well-being.

Listening and Reading for Understanding

- Differentiate between informal and formal exchanges.
- Comprehend phrases related to a person's state of well-being.

Oral and Written Presentation

- Demonstrate attention to accuracy of register in introducing self and expressing greetings.
- Present rehearsed and spontaneous greetings and introductions.

Cultures

Cultural Perspectives, Practices, and Products

- Recognize and distinguish between various culturally authentic gestures and levels of formality of greeting and leave-taking.
- Demonstrate understanding of hand-shaking, body language, and greetings, including those used in telephone, computer, and letter-writing situations.

Connections, Comparisons, and Communities

Making Connections through Language

- Discuss the use of morning and evening greetings.

Cultural and Linguistic Comparisons

- Contrast customs of greeting and leave-taking between the United States and Spanish speaking countries. Contrast the use of formal address in Spanish and English.

Communication across Communities

- Recognize the importance of greetings in Spanish-speaking countries.

When teachers write goals like these, students, parents, and administrators know what the expected outcomes are. It is very important to have lesson plans that mirror these goals as well as assessments. It is recommended to visit websites of other districts to see if course descriptions, course syllabi, and goals are posted so that you can have samples to use to develop your own goals.

Lesson Plan Writing

Planning for instruction is one of the most important keys to success in the classroom. Reflective teachers take into consideration the progress made by students in previous lessons and plan carefully for the next steps. It is important to distinguish between an agenda or itinerary, (i.e., a list of activities that you plan to do) and a lesson plan that identifies key outcomes in terms of student learning.

At the end of the lesson planning process, teachers should be able to answer the following questions:

- How is this lesson aligned with the state and national foreign language standards?
- How does your lesson encourage your students to take responsibility for their own learning?
- How will your students use their knowledge to solve authentic, real-life situations?
- How do your activities provide ways for your students to demonstrate their learning?
- How will you evaluate the effectiveness of your lesson?

In developing a lesson plan, be sure to:

- Identify the language and level for the lesson.
- Note the theme and topic for the lesson.
- List the resources that will be used to implement the lesson.
- Identify the standards that the lesson will address.
- Indicate the learning objectives.
- Explain the design of the activities describing what students will do and how the learning will take place, such as paired activities or small groups.
- Have students reflect on what they have learned. Many teachers select a student at the end of class to summarize what he/she has learned. This can be done as a full class or in small groups. It helps students take on the responsibility for managing their own learning. Other teachers have students keep journals and at the end of the period they have students write their thoughts or a brief summary of what they have learned. It is also a recommended to have students give examples of what they have learned as a way of proving what they have learned as a result of the lesson.

- Explain how the teacher will assess the students' performance and/or acquired knowledge.

If you prepare yourself by thinking through every aspect of lesson implementation and desired student outcomes before entering the classroom, you'll probably be able to convey to your students why they are doing what you are asking of them, and how it fits in the larger picture. And you'll be able to assess their performance and pinpoint sections of the lesson that may need to be re-addressed. A well-developed lesson also reduces the probability that you will teach a grammatical structure simply because it comes next in the chapter, or assign students to do a textbook exercise simply because it falls under the grammar point that was just introduced.

At the end of each lesson planning process be sure to note in your plan book what worked well and what might need to be changed for the next year. This will save you time in future years.

Assessments

Assessing student achievement in a standards-based classroom means that students will be assessed more frequently on what they can do in the language rather than what they know about the language. This means that open-ended performance tasks will be administered periodically so that students can be assessed on their progress.

We have long known that students study or pay attention to what they feel they will be tested on. A common question you'll get from students when you introduce a topic is, "Will we be tested on this?" In other words, "Do we have to learn this?" But teachers often play the same game, when they announce, "Listen carefully to what I am teaching you today because you are going to be tested on this on Friday." What both the teacher and the student are doing is categorizing portions of a lesson as "important" and "not important."

Since assessments should always mirror instruction, teachers should assess for student proficiency rather than for isolated vocabulary words or discrete verb forms. If the goal of teaching a foreign language is to have students communicate and interpret in the target language, teachers should assess their students to see if they can indeed use the vocabulary and verb forms in context in order to communicate thoughts and ideas.

Many educators have embraced the standards-based model for instruction and teachers are being asked to write standards-based lesson plans, but time and again teachers fall back on the selected-response test format with the opinion that it is faster to grade and "more accurate" in terms of a definite answer without arguments.

But if you are going to look at the big picture when you plan a lesson, ask yourself, "What is it I want the students to be able to do at the end of this lesson?" Then use your district's measurement tool or design a measurement tool that indicates all of what the students can do at the end of the lesson, not merely what they have memorized and were able to recognize briefly during the test. Performance assessments can take longer to grade, but when you get comfortable using a rubric, the pace of grading each assessment picks up. It is important to note that teachers should use a variety of assessments and a balance in terms of types of assessments. This means that not every type of assessment needs to be used in every unit.

In order to develop an assessment system that truly monitors students' progress in developing communicative competence, consider these strategies for managing performance assessment:

- Give a performance assessment in lieu of a chapter test. If the students understand the rubric and what it is you expect them to be able to do, they should be able to show you what they have learned in a much more meaningful way than filling in blanks on a form.
- Consider dividing the performance assessments up by units and assessing oral communication in one unit and written communication in the next.
- Similarly, divide assessments by levels or class periods, for example odd period classes one week, even the next. If you assess all students on one day, the grading is overwhelming and it will take longer to get the results back to your students. Feedback to students is what makes a rubric much better than simply a grade as an indicator of student progress and areas that need improvement. If your students don't get feedback from you in a timely fashion, they'll have more difficulty knowing where they need to improve before the next assessment.
- Don't feel that you have to correct every mistake. Simply highlight errors and ask students to make corrections for additional grade points. Some students do not digest all the comments teachers write on the papers anyway. If students are taught how to analyze their mistakes and make revi-

sions, on their own or with a peer, this will increase their capacity to self-correct.

- Periodically replace a traditional quiz or two with a formative* writing task. As long as the task is well-written (with clear objectives, minimum requirements, and a scenario to set the scene) students should be able to show you how much they have learned.

Organizing for Efficiency

At the end of your first year of teaching, you'll probably say that next year you need to be better organized. You may ask veteran colleagues for tips. Even long-time teachers admit this is an area in which they are still discovering new "tricks of the trade." All teachers seem to agree that a major hassle is handling all the paperwork. The following tips may help you get and stay organized. Teachers should:

- Have a place set up (either on a cart or in the classroom) for "in-coming" and "out-going" student papers. This can be in the form of file folders by class period positioned in file holders, baskets that are labeled, accordion folders, "in" and "out" boxes, whatever you prefer.
- Have a similar set-up for handouts to students. Always keep a few extra handouts in each file so you can access them easily when students have been absent or misplace their copy. Keep appropriate handouts in the easily accessible file for the duration of the unit.
- Backup all handouts to a CD or flash drive and post them to the school's server, a course management system like Blackboard, a website, or an area where students can access the copies without having to ask you. This puts the responsibility on the students to secure their materials. Parents who have access to these sites can also see what has been handed out and stay up-to-date with the instruction.
- Post a calendar of special events, quizzes, tests, and project due dates in the class or on a mobile cart, and ask students to record the dates in a student calendar. If you have access to a course management system, also keep the information posted online so students and parents can stay aware.
- Keep a notebook of transparencies near the overhead projector. Label dividers so that a particular transparency can be located in a hurry.

* A formative task is more specific and has the students perform on a topic that has recently been learned. This type of task is general used at the end of a lesson or unit. A summative task is very general. This type of task is used at the end of the year and students are asked to show what they have learned, which can include several topics.

- Have a folder in a briefcase or satchel for make-up quizzes or tests. On the day of the assessment, write the name of any student who is absent on a copy of the quiz or test you distributed, date it, and put it in the folder. That way, you'll be able to locate the quiz quickly when the student comes in after school to make it up. This will also serve to remind you if the student fails to come in and make up the quiz in a timely manner.
- Maintain a calendar to remember scheduled conferences, parent requests for a progress report, faculty meetings, due dates for interims, and everything else you are responsible for. It's best to use a calendar on your computer; many of them have a reminder option. If you don't have access to a PC, set up a notebook-style calendar.
- Keep a phone log. Keep a notebook next to your phone, and every time you call a parent, it should be recorded, with a brief note of the subject and a call-back reminder if required. This will also assist your record-keeping for parent conferences, school meetings, and the like.
- Routines help keep you organized. If you always do certain things on certain days, it's easier to remember—for example, tutor on Mondays and Wednesdays, attend meetings on Tuesdays, offer make-up assessments on Thursdays. Leave Friday afternoons for planning the next week.
- Ask a different student in each class to keep a record of everything that is done during class on that day. Maintain a three ring binder for each class with these pages. Expect absent students to check the binder for information about what was missed. Extra copies of handouts can also be kept in the binder for absent students.

Back-to-School Night

This will be your first formal meeting with parents. It's an important night for you. The impression you make on the parents of your students on this early fall evening will set the tone for the year. Since middle school and high school students have anywhere from six to seven teachers, parents are usually given a schedule for their visit to each class, with travel time allowed in between. This allows them only about 10 minutes in each class, not counting allowing time for parents who get lost and arrive late. So it is extremely important to have this time well organized in order to maximize every minute of your time with the parents. Before the big night, send home with your students a Welcome Parents kit with:

- The student's schedule
- A map of the school with the foreign language class well marked

- The bell schedule for that evening
- Your talking points for the 10 minutes
- Contact information, so parents can contact you with any questions they may have that cannot be addressed that evening.
- A note to parents that this evening is not a time to discuss issues specific to their student, but also information on how they may set up a parent/teacher conference with you if they want to discuss their student's progress in a private setting.

It goes without saying that you should pay special attention to the way you dress for this occasion. Professional attire is critical to assure parents that you take this job very seriously. Your appearance speaks louder than words. If a professional looks sloppy, most people fear that the service they receive will be sub-par. This is especially important if you are right out of college and only four or five years older than your students.

Prior to the parents' arrival, set up your classroom to look inviting and make sure all of the equipment you will use in your presentation is in working order. Use the tips below to keep your meeting on schedule:

- Have a sign-in sheet outside the door for parents to write their names and their child's name.
- Have the agenda on the board, on an overhead transparency or a PowerPoint slide, for parents to see as they enter the classroom and get seated.
- Have a portion of a video/DVD being used in class showing as parents enter the room. This allows parents to hear a bit of the language and allows them to experience just how different foreign language classes are today.
- Give each parent a 3x5 index card as they enter so that they can jot down a question about something you did not cover in your presentation or to make a note about something they feel you should know about their child. (This facilitates communication with parents while preventing specific student-related questions from bogging down your program).
- Distribute a Back-to-School Night brochure or handout containing all your talking points so parents do not feel they have to take detailed notes during your presentation.

During your presentation be sure to address the following:

Objectives. Parents should know what their child will be able to do by the end of the year at that level.

Available courses. What courses will be available the following year or the sequence of courses that are recommended.

Resources. Show parents what the textbook looks like and explain how all the ancillaries will aid in student learning. This is also a good time to discuss how technology will be used to enhance classroom instruction.

Classroom rules and teacher expectations. Explain briefly your grading policy and how parents can help monitor their child's progress. Remind parents of the policies that were sent home at the beginning of the year and encourage them to contact you if they have questions.

Progress reports. Tell parents when they can expect to be notified of their child's progress—for example, if a student: 1) drops one letter grade; 2) fails a major test; 3) does not turn in three assignments; 4) fails to get an interim report signed; 5) does not pick up a weekly progress report that was requested by the parent.

Study strategies. Give parents tips on effective study strategies so they can assist in ensuring their students' progress.

And since these talking points probably will take up most of your time, be sure you remind parents how they can contact you whenever they have additional questions.

Make-up Work

When teachers have more than 100 students in their charge, staying on top of make-up work can alone be an arduous task. You should have a policy for making up homework assignments, quizzes, projects, and tests. Make your policy clear to students and parents during the first week of school and reinforce it during the first marking period. Your policy should include:

- How a student can obtain the assignment if absent.
- When a student can come after school to take a make-up assessment.
- A deadline for make-up work and details about how many class sessions the student is allowed to make up work after each absence. Note: If a school is on block scheduling, it can be confusing to state how many "days" a student has, because the class meets every other day.
- A deadline for extended absences. If a student has been out for a week or longer, you should communicate a plan to enable the student to get the work in—keeping in mind the student also has 5-6 other classes of make-up work.
- Your expectation of the student and the consequence if a project deadline is missed due to an absence.
- The consequence for not making up work.

When assigning make-up work for an extended absence, keep in mind that some assignments could be shortened or eliminated. For example, if the student can learn a particular language structure after one 10-sentence exercise, then perhaps the other four similar exercises can be omitted. For a two or three-week absence, it's important to look at the long-range objectives and reconsider and revise the daily homework exercises. It is important that the student feels he or she can keep up with this class along with his or her other classes. Perhaps a tutor can be recommended or after-school sessions can be set up when the student returns to make sure certain elements have been learned.

Parent/Teacher Conferences

Probably the most important piece of advice you could receive about these conferences is this: Parent conferences are much more productive if you have made contact with the parent in a positive sense prior to the meeting. Starting the year on a positive note usually develops an atmosphere of collaboration with the parent.

It is always a good strategy to contact the parent of a student who may need extra help to mention the good things he or she is doing in class and perhaps suggest one additional strategy that may make things even better. If you feel another phone call or e-mail is necessary, the second contact should also be in the format of offering helpful suggestions. You could also mention to the parent a particular strategy that may have worked in the past or the fact that you noticed that the student was much better prepared because of the extra effort given in doing the homework assignment.

If a parent requests a conference because the student is not showing progress or his or her work is actually declining, your tone should be helpful, such as "Let's brainstorm some ways to help Johnny succeed," rather than placing blame.

On the day of the conference, be at the meeting site on time and fully prepared to discuss the student's performance. Come to the conference armed with the following:

- **A list of the student's grades and a current average** for the marking period as of the day of the conference. Be sure you have graded any work that the student has made up or has completed, even if the work from the other students has not yet been graded.
- **Samples of the student's work.** If you want the parent to understand that the student's work is always incomplete, then it is much more effective to show the parent a sample of an actual incomplete assignment or show examples of the student's short or incomplete answers on a test. Often students tell parents what they think parents want to hear. Anything the teacher can share with a parent will help the student's performance in the long run.
- **Attendance record.** If attendance (or late arrivals to class) is the problem, have all of the student's "absent" dates listed. Any make-up work that hasn't been turned in should also be listed so that the parent is fully informed and can help get the student "back on track."
- **A recommended plan of action.** A parent is taking the time to come in and talk to you because he or she is concerned about the child's progress. The parent wants to leave with a sense of hope that things will turn around. If you can work with the parent on strategies that both you and the parent can follow and a plan for the student to take responsibility for his or her learning, the parent probably will leave with the feeling that the school is just as concerned about this student as the parent is. The plan should include:
  - How you will communicate with the parent
  - A date for the next conference.
  - Measurable goals and objectives for the student
  - Strategies to help the student meet these goals
  - An evaluation design—How the parent and you will know these goals have been met.
- **Recommended resources.** Some parents are at a complete loss on how to help their child. So be prepared to give the parent information on local tutors, Internet tutorials, outside resources such as books, CDs, movies, games in the target language, and peer tutoring information, in which language honor society students help the student.
- **Include the student in the conference.** It is always a good idea to include the student in the conference. It is important for both the student and the parent to hear the same message from you and vice versa. It also helps establish the "team" approach to helping the student improve.
- **Have a counselor present.** Most schools have a policy that the counselor must be present at the conference. For the first several years of teaching, it's important that you insist on this. Counselors can be helpful if the conference becomes contentious and it's important for you to have a third party present.

Classroom Management

If you are having classroom management problems, ask yourself the following questions:

- Do I make my expectations clear or are students trying to guess what is on my mind?
- Do I give the students too much time to complete a particular assignment?
- Are my lessons interesting and relevant?
- Do my students understand why they are doing a particular activity?
- Have I changed activities often enough during a class period?
- Are my lesson objectives clearly stated and posted where students can see them?
- Are my students saying that they hate "busy work"?
- Am I consistent in implementing classroom rules?
- Do students consider me a figure of authority or a friend?
- Do I follow through with consequences for students?
- Have I earned the respect of my students?
- Do I follow my own rules?

Many veteran teachers have learned that when they use well-written lessons with a variety of activities, they have fewer classroom management issues. Students want to know what they are going to learn today and if it is important down the road. Always explain the big picture to students and let them know how today's lesson fits into that program.

For example, you might explain to your students that it is very important to learn certain vocabulary words and how they are used in forming questions and answers, because in a week they are going to be sitting in a classroom "restaurant" ordering a meal. When it registers that without today's lesson on essential vocabulary they may not get to eat, they will digest anything the teacher hands out! All lessons may not be as appetizing for them, but they'll surely get the point that learning brings rewards, and that you aren't giving them a particular exercise just because it comes next in the textbook.

Another secret to classroom discipline is setting the stage for respect. As long as there is mutual respect, and students see you as the authority figure, not a peer, then the structure of the class should be obvious. If you explain the consequence of breaking a class rule and then do not follow through with students who do, you will lose the respect of your class. It is sometimes difficult to reprimand a "good" student, but if you don't treat every student the same way, you could face a rebellion later on. Students want teachers to be fair. They often do not object to the rules, but they will be quick to lose trust in teachers who let some students get away with things that others cannot.

Communicating Beyond the Classroom

It is important to be able to communicate with parents and the community at large about the foreign language program and perhaps other issues at your school. It would be great if such communication was always supportive. But there are times when you may be confronted with negative comments or questions about your school or program. If that happens to you, don't panic. Stay calm. Then consider carefully how you will respond. Here are a few tips to help you deal with such situations:

To whom will you be responding?

- Shape your response with awareness and consideration of the person or group you are addressing.
- Take into account your addressee's apparent knowledge of the issue at hand. See if you can discover how detailed the dialogue is likely to be, with respect to the person's vocabulary, experience, and language ability.

How much does the constituency know about the subject?

- Did the person or persons get information from a student, neighbor, friend?
- If the correspondence is in writing via a letter or e-mail, it is especially important to respond in kind and with care. Treat your correspondent with integrity and respect no matter how hot the issue.

What was the purpose of the original communication?

- Be sure you understand the question.
- Are legal ramifications likely?
- What is the context of this communication? Are there undercurrents? Is this an attempt to discredit you or a staff member?
- Be aware of the respondent's slant or point of view. Listen or look for phrases, such as "in my opinion," or vague words such as "people," "peers," or "groups."
- What seems to be the key source of the concern or hostility?
- Always respond to your correspondent with a sincere, straightforward, and tactful answer.

Crafting a response

- Is your response an acknowledgement?
- Are you providing information, explanation, and/or clarification?
- Are you responding to defend department policy?
- Do not write or respond verbally while you are angry.
- Put the message aside, take time to think about your response, leave your personal emotion out of the response. Aim to defuse the situation.
- Never use sarcasm.
- Do not state facts you cannot defend.

Style and tone

- Use a clear and concise writing style, imparting clear ideas in a few words.
- Eliminate extra words or superfluous information.
- Impart ideas briefly and in a straightforward way.
- How can the data be presented fairly? Find neutral ground.
- Be sure to address the heart of the matter. If you're not sure about it, ask colleagues and supervisors for help.

Closing remarks

- Be firm, but professional.
- Close on a positive note, thanking the writer for expressing his or her viewpoint.
- Display a true sense of concern—and an offer of help.

Instructional Time: Use Every Minute

It takes a while to get the timing down for a 50-minute class, and it is especially tricky to plan for a 90-minute class on block scheduling. The key to using every minute is to have a couple of extra activities planned in case you discover there are 20 empty minutes at the end of the lesson. In such cases, some teachers tell students they can use the last 10 minutes to complete their homework.

However, this often signals to students that class "is over," and students feel free to chat and relax. In a 90-minute class students are tired and this 10-minute "start your homework" strategy ends up being counterproductive. Very few students want to dive in and get as much done as humanly possible. To the contrary, by the time they get all their materials out to start on homework, they find there isn't enough time to complete it, so why start? Talking is more fun. Instead, use the following activities to fill those 10- or 20-minute gaps at the end of a lesson:

- Divide the class in groups and see which group is first to come up with "The five things we learned today."
- Require students to write in a journal at the end of each lesson a reflection of what they learned today.
- Toss a nerf ball around the class, allowing each student who catches it to ask another student what he learned in today's lesson. Divide the class in two teams and keep a running count of points for each team. At the end of the week or month, the team with the most points gets bonus points on a quiz.
- Have blank comic strips handy and have students fill in the blank bubbles with a conversation.
- Have students pick scenario cards and come in front of the class to act out a scene.
- From a box of stuffed animals, baseball cards, goofy trinkets, and the like, have students pick a "show and tell" item and tell the class why it is so special to them, or make up a story about it.

Activities such as these have no grades attached and are a good way to end a class on a positive note. Students leave feeling like they have learned something and/or have performed spontaneously without the pressure of making a mistake. These are great closing activities to build self-esteem and keep the momentum going until time is up.

Student Recognition

Know this: students love attention, be it negative or positive. Never forget the power of positive attention and the results that can come from it. There are students sitting in every classroom who go through the system with little or no recognition year after year. They do not have the stellar grades, athletic talent, or popularity of students often in the limelight. They do not have discipline issues that some students do. They do what they are told and ask for very little in return. Yet they watch the same students win awards and receive recognition time and time again.

Don't take the quiet disposition of these students for granted, thinking they are doing what is expected of them and forgetting to reward them for their accomplishments as good classroom citizens. The real reward of teaching is to give such students positive attention and watch them blossom. Recognize students who:

- Bring their books to class every day for a marking period.
- Cooperate in group work activities every time.
- Come to class on time every day.
- Have perfect attendance for a marking period.
- Share materials with a classmate who forgets to bring something.
- Exhibit the most effort on their work.
- Are the most improved.
- Actively participate in class several days in a row.
- Volunteer to help a classmate.
- Help decorate a bulletin board.
- Follow all class rules.

Ideas for recognition:

- A pencil imprinted with a slogan in the target language
- Appreciation certificate
- Recognition stickers
- Recognition beads (to add on a belt or necklace)
- Fake coins that can be collected and "cashed in" for reward at the end of a marking period
- Posting the student's name on a recognition board (such as "Student of the Week")

An especially powerful way to reward a student is to call attention in class to his or her activity beyond the foreign language classroom. For example, give students credit for performance in sporting events, plays, choral concerts, debate team presentations, or artwork in an exhibit. If a student isn't excelling in your language course, it doesn't necessarily follow that he or she does not excel in another area. It means so much for students to know that their teacher came to see their accomplishments in another discipline or extra-curricular activity. Often when students feel their teacher cares about them in this way, they will put forth a little more effort so as not to disappoint the teacher. Positive attention wins respect and can turn a student around. It is always a treat when a graduate comes back to visit and tells the teacher that a particular act on the teacher's part meant so much.

Connections with Students

It's important to find out what makes your students tick. In the first month of school you have the opportunity to ask students many questions to get them back into speaking the target language. As a warm-up exercise, ask questions that allow you to learn what students like to do in their free time, their favorite movies, books, sports, pets, food, and the like. Some teachers have students create a collage describing all this information about them, with their photo in the middle. This usually opens up communication, lets students know a little more about each other, and gives you valuable insight into each student's world. If you expect students to really communicate with one another, it's important that they get to know each other and learn to care about one another. One teacher using this technique wrote each student's likes and dislikes on a seating chart. In classroom sessions, her students couldn't believe how much their teacher remembered about each of them through the year!

Letters and Endorsements for Students

You will be asked at various times to time to write letters of recommendation for students. You may also need to write thank you letters, invitations to school events, commendations, and responses to parent concerns. Over the years many teachers develop a file of letters that they can use as templates for new drafts of letters and documents.

As a new teacher, writing letters may seem a daunting task at first. How should you begin your letter? How much should you write? What should be included? This handbook includes letter templates for many situations. They are meant to jump-start the process for you. Modifications will definitely be needed, but the templates will save you considerable time. As a rule of thumb, keep letters short. Get to your point early on. Keep letters to one page if at all possible. Here are some tips about formatting letters to make them clear and precise:

- Include an opening statement and orientation, in which you:
  - State the reason for the letter.
  - Acknowledge a previous letter.
  - Provide specific information.

- In the body of the letter, you should:
  - Explain background details. In the case of an invitation to an event, describe the sponsoring organization and the significance of the event.
  - In a recommendation, cite specific examples to back up your positive remarks.
  - In response to a parental concern, clarify what action has been taken and any further steps proposed.

- Be sure your letter:
  - Displays empathy with your correspondent, so he or she will feel that you have taken his or her feelings into account.
  - Backs up what you have said with details and other references.
  - Specifically asks the person to take specific action.
  - Thanks the person in advance for being willing to comply with your request, and for his or her effort and time in the endeavor.

Remember, letters should be saved. Create a file for them. You can use them for proof of participation, to answer routine questions, to prepare responses (with a few modifications) to requests you receive from individuals and organizations. Of course, always proofread your letters very carefully, and don't write anything that you can't back up with documentation.

Special Needs Students

The purpose of this section is to help you create classroom environments that will enhance foreign language instruction and meet the needs of **all** students. There are specific strategies that will augment the learning of students who may need additional help. You should contact your school district's Office of Special Education or meet with a special education teacher at your school to learn about the variety of strategies that should be used to help special education students succeed in the classroom, even while they cope with specific processing difficulties or disabilities.

The Individuals with Disabilities Education Act Amendments (IDEA, 1977) encourage the inclusion of children with disabilities in the least restrictive environment (LRE) to the maximum extent appropriate with children who are not disabled. These laws and regulations change, so take the initiative early on to visit the numerous websites where current information regarding special education can be found. All general education teachers, including foreign language teachers, may access support from special education staff members at their schools. A special education teacher should contact the foreign language teacher early in the year regarding the special education students in class. However, if you are not contacted by special ed people, pursue contact on your own initiative. You need to become aware of special ed accommodations early in the school year, preferably early enough to implement any accommodations needed before Back-to-School Night.

Foreign language teachers should express special education-related concerns and questions to the case manager or special education department. Foreign language teachers may be asked to participate in Individualized Education Program (IEP) meetings. This process varies from school to school, both in frequency and format. You are advised to keep documentation and copies of all information you received on this subject. You may participate in the IEP process of any of your students, regardless of whether or not this participation has been formally requested. In addition, you or a parent may request an IEP meeting at any time to address possible changes to accommodations and services.

Accommodations are legally binding.

All teachers must implement, document, and adapt classroom materials and/or environment as identified within the IEP and the 504 plan, including making accommodations for assessments. If necessary, you should seek assistance to implement accommodations as written and stay in contact with staff members, parents, and students regarding progress. You must keep documentation (i.e., work samples) that demonstrates each student's progress and use of accommodations. Parents have the right to request such documentation at any time. Even though there are many strategies specific to certain processing difficulties, there are some basic strategies that you can use not only with special education students, but with your class as a whole.

Basic classroom strategies:

- Talk to students honestly about the task of learning a language, the work involved, and the rewards to be gained.
- Create a classroom climate in which students feel comfortable and involved.
- Help students develop the art of inference by making them aware of clues for intelligent guessing.
- Personalize instruction in order to motivate students to express themselves readily.
- Ask students to monitor each other's speech and thus take an active part not only in learning but also in teaching.
- Seek opportunities for students to use the language outside the classroom.
- Present all material in a meaningful context and manner.
- Ask successful language learners to serve as informants regarding strategies, techniques, and study skills.
- Encourage learners with special needs to experiment freely until they find their own particular learning style.

Classroom participation:

- To encourage spontaneous oral communication, avoid overcorrection, a practice that tends to inhibit students' attempts to speak the language.
- Include age-appropriate situations and questions in daily speaking practices.
- Allow students to earn credit:
  - For frequency and accuracy of responses.
  - For warm-up activities, worksheets done in class, partner practices, role-playing activities, and cooperative learning activities.
  - For attempted responses given in the target language, regardless of correctness.

Teacher Evaluation and Observations

Most school systems have established procedures for teacher evaluation. It is important to find out early in the year what those procedures are and to know how you will be evaluated. Generally, there is a goal-setting conference early in the year with your evaluator and this will be an opportunity for you to ask questions about the process. You can always ask your department chair about how the process will work in your school.

You may be asked to provide the following information regarding your lesson:

- National, State, and Local Standards
- Planning and Assessment
- Instruction
- Learning Environment

Develop lesson plans to include:

- Communication—Interpersonal, Interpretive, and Presentational Modes
- Cultures
- Connections
- Comparisons
- Communities

Plan lessons that:

- integrate listening, speaking, reading, and writing into the three modes of communication
- are student-centered, which includes working independently, in pairs, or in groups.
- recognize a diverse student population.
- include a variety of learning modes.
- provide opportunities for practice.
- are aligned with the district's curriculum guide and are not textbook driven.

If you have a pre-observation conference:

- Tell observer what you expect the students to learn at the end of the unit.
- Explain what students have learned in the previous lesson.
- Explain what role this lesson plays to achieving the "end result."
- Show the observer what you have planned for the next lesson.
- Make sure you indicate how your lesson is aligned with the National Standards.
- Indicate how students will be assessed.

What administrators may look for:

- You and the students should speak the target language throughout the lesson in Levels 1 through Upper Level.
- Students should be speaking the language at every opportunity. Student performance is the focus.
- Use visual cues instead of English to enhance student learning.
- Let the textbook be a resource and not the sole source of information.
- Use a variety of strategies to meet the needs of all learners.
- Students should be practicing with partners as often as possible. A noisy class is not a bad class.
- Assess students often in a variety of ways, formally and informally.
- Use technology to enhance learning.

Learning Environment:

- There must be a positive classroom climate.
- Students must feel it's "safe" to make a mistake.
- Students must show respect toward other students and allow for mistakes.
- Desks are arranged to allow for communication.
- Students feel no question is a dumb question and participation is encouraged.
- Teachers encourage students constantly.

Assessments:

You should…

- assess what has been learned in the class.
- assess frequently and in a variety of ways.
- administer formative performance assessments.
- administer summative performance assessments.

Am I Ready?

☐ I have prepared my **goals and objectives** for the marking period and school year.
- ☐ I have asked a member of my department to proof my course goals and give me feedback.
- ☐ My goals have been approved by the appropriate administrator.

☐ I have prepared **lesson plans** that include:
- ☐ Course title and course code
- ☐ The language and level for the lesson
- ☐ Theme and topic for the lesson
- ☐ Resources that will be used to implement the lesson
- ☐ Standards that the lesson will address
- ☐ The learning objectives
- ☐ The design of the activities
- ☐ Reflection
- ☐ Assessment

☐ I have developed a variety of formal and informal **assessments** to measure student learning.

☐ I am **organized**
- ☐ I have a place set up for student papers.
- ☐ I have a plan in place for storing handouts so that I can access them easily when students have been absent.
- ☐ I have backed up all handouts and have posted them online or have them stored in a binder for students to access at a later time.
- ☐ I have a calendar posted for special events, assessments, and projects.
- ☐ I have a notebook of transparencies near the overhead projector.
- ☐ I have a calendar to record conferences, meetings, parent requests, etc.
- ☐ I have a notebook set up for a phone log.

☐ I have developed a **Back-to-School** handout or brochure for parents.

☐ I have developed a **make-up work** policy.

☐ I am prepared for **parent conferences** and know to bring with me the following:
- ☐ A list of the student's grades and a current average for the marking period as of the day of the conference
- ☐ Samples of the student's work
- ☐ Attendance record
- ☐ A recommended Plan of Action
- ☐ A date I am free in case the parents want a follow-up conference

- ☐ I have a well-developed plan for **classroom management.**
  - ☐ My expectations are clear.
  - ☐ I have every minute accounted for in my lesson plan so there is no down-time.
  - ☐ My lessons are interesting and relevant.
  - ☐ My students understand why they are doing a particular activity.
  - ☐ I include several activities in each lesson.
  - ☐ My lesson objectives are clearly stated and posted where students can see them.
  - ☐ I avoid the use of "busy work."
  - ☐ I implement the same classroom rules consistently.
  - ☐ Students consider me a figure of authority.
  - ☐ I follow through with consequences for students.
  - ☐ I have the respect of my students.
  - ☐ I follow my own rules.

- ☐ I have a plan to **communicate** regularly with parents.

- ☐ I have a **pacing guide.**

- ☐ I plan to **recognize students** for not only achievement, but also effort and success outside of the classroom.

Reflection

What aspect of this chapter worked well?

What would I change for next year?

How would I change it?

What additional resources do I need to gather for next year?

Template J | Standards-Based Unit Design with Assessment Tasks

German III • Unit 5
Travel

STAGE ONE:
What Students Should Know and Be Able To Do

Essential Question:
How is traveling in a German-speaking country different from traveling in the United States?

What students should be able to do:

Elements (These elements can be derived from a state framework or district curriculum)
Express needs and desires
Exchange opinions and preferences
Ask questions and provide responses based on suggested topics
Begin to participate in an oral or written exchange reflecting future and past tenses
Demonstrate Novice-High to Intermediate-Low proficiency in oral and written exchanges
Understand culturally authentic materials and information
Participate in real or simulated cultural events

What students should know:

- Beginning use of future tense (verb "*werden*" = will) in both conversation and writing
- Beginning use of present perfect tense in both conversation and writing
- Use of informal commands
- Use of transition words to connect sentences/paragraphs
- Use of opinions about likes/dislikes
- Prepositions related to travel:
- *zu* vs. *nach* (when to use *zu* for "to" and *nach* for "to" in German)
- *mit* (use for "with" for transportation in German)
- 2-way prepositions-*in/an/auf* (when to use the different words for "at" in German) Vocabulary related to: modes of transportation, directions, accommodations, sightseeing
- Verbs of travel: *reisen* (to travel), *fahren* (to drive or travel), *besuchen* (to visit), *besichtigen* (to sightsee or visit), *nehmen* (to take), *bleiben* (to stay or remain), *packen* (to pack), *brauchen* (to need)

STAGE TWO:
How Students Evidence What They Know and Can Do

Performance-Based Assessment 1

When will we arrive?

Student Task:
You and your family are going to spend three weeks in Berlin with some German friends of yours. Since you are the only one in your family who speaks German, you have to write an e-mail to your friends to let them know when to expect you. You need to tell them the following information: which airline you will use, which flight you will be on, which airport you will fly into, date and time of your arrival, and date and time of your departure.

Summative Performance Based Assessment 2

Which youth hostel should we choose?

Student Task:
You and your best friend want to experience staying in a youth hostel while in Germany. You want to know some details about one that a German teenager recommended. Call the youth hostel manager for the Jugendherberge Wandlitz and find out the following: how to get there from Berlin, how much it costs per night, what meals are included or are optional, and what activities are available. Make a reservation for two beds. Use this link for the hostel: *http://www.jugendherberge.de/de/jugendherbergen/visitenkarte/jh.jsp?IDJH=623*. You will role-play the young person asking questions, and your teacher or a classmate will be the manager of the hostel. You may jot down some vocabulary words in German to prompt your responses.

Summative Performance Based Assessment 3

How do I get around on the metro?

Student Task:
You want to see some of the famous sights in Berlin. You will be using public transportation to get around and you do not use it very often in America. For this reason you want to get directions to trace your route in advance on a metro map. Ask a German working at the train station to help you. Use the map located at this website: *www.fahrinfo-berlin.de/gis/index.jsp*. You must begin at the Zoologischer Garten stop since it's very close to where you are staying. Your first sights are at Unter den Linden and then you will have further stops at Potsdamer Platz, Wittenbergplatz, and Kurfürstendamm before you return to the Zoologischer Garten. Before you begin your day, take a look at the list of sights you can see at the stops and choose what you want to see ahead of time. (See this link for ideas: *http://www.berlin-tourist-information.de/english/sightseeing/e_si_berlinprogramme.php*.) You will visit at least six different places. The person giving directions may make notes in English on his/her copy of the map. The conversation may be recorded or presented to the teacher.

Teacher Note: You can substitute any other format of a metro map (from textbook, overhead, etc.) for a German-speaking city. Just select a route you want the students to follow and suggest places they could see along the route.

Summative Performance Based Assessment 4

How would I describe my sightseeing trip?

Student Task:
After your day seeing the sights of Berlin, you want to write to your German teacher back home and tell her about what you saw. In your letter, describe at least three sights you visited in detail. Tell what your favorite sight was and why. Also, tell her if there was anything you did not enjoy. Try to impress your teacher with your use of past tense!

STAGE THREE:
Instructional Activities That Help Students Know and Be Able To Do Interdisciplinary Instructional Tasks

Interpersonal Communicative Tasks

1. Let's go to Germany! (Social Studies, Math)
You and a friend are going to fly from Atlanta to Hamburg and back. You want to stay for two weeks. Your German grandparents must approve your travel choice because they are paying for the trip. You have to discuss it with them in German. Go to the Lufthansa website: *http://konzern.lufthansa.com/de/index.html.* Enter a departure and arrival date and print out your possible flight choices. Discuss with your partner in German which flight to take, how much it costs in Euros/dollars, when you will leave, and when you will come back home.

2. How do we get around Muenchen? (Social Studies)
You are in Muenchen, a city you know well, and a German from a small town asks you for directions to some famous sights. Looking at a map of the old city (Altstadt) part of Muenchen, give your partner (the German) directions to three sights. Begin at the city hall (Neues Rathaus). Use a map you have or try this map: *http://www.hotmaps.de/europe/germany/bavaria/munich/homeen.html.*
Teacher Note: This works well if you give one student an end point where they must direct their partner and have the student check at the end to see if their partner ended up at the right point.

3. What did I miss? (Social Studies)
You and your German cousin, who speaks little English, both explored part of Frankfurt together. Then you decided to split up because you wanted to see different things. Ask each other what you saw and describe two places you visited without each other. Use this website to pick two authentic places: *http://www.visit-germany.info/web/en_uk/top50/index.htm?tl=STADT&showid=1078.* You can also just make up names for fictitious places that are likely to be in any city of that size such as a museum or a theater.

4. Where should I go? (Social Studies)
You work part-time in a travel agency in Germany and your partner is a customer. He cannot decide where to go on vacation in Germany. You need to convince him to go to a specific area that you like. Suggest an area and then give reasons why he should go there. Your partner should respond to your suggestions with questions to get more information from you. You should have at least five exchanges.

5. Can you follow my directions? (Social Studies)
With a partner, create a basic town square map on a piece of paper with four streets, streetlights, a stop sign, a railroad crossing, etc. Draw three or four generic buildings on each street. Make two copies of the map so each person has the identical map. The first partner should tell the other where to begin and then give directions to three different buildings. For example: Begin at the stop sign on Mozart Street. Go straight until the street light and then turn left. At the corner on the left side of the street is the bank building. As the directions are given, the partner follows them and labels each building. Switch roles and then check each other's maps to see if they are still the same.

Interpretive Communicative Tasks

6. Plane, train, or automobile? (Social Studies, Art, Physical Education)
Have students work in pairs to list as many modes of transportation as they can in English. Then have one student call out to the partner a mode of transportation from the list in German while the partner draws a picture of it to show that he knows the word. This could also be done as a whole class activity if you play Win, Lose, or Draw on the board up front.

7. How much does that cost in euros? (Social Studies, Math)
You and your family are going to Europe. You have $1,000 dollars to spend on a hotel for a week in Bavaria. You need to find out the current conversion rate for dollars to euros. Go to this website: *http://www.xe.com/ucc/*. Once you determine how many euros you have, find a hotel you can afford online. You can try this site: *http://www.deutschland-tourismus.de/DEU/infocenter/unterkuenfte.htm*. Be prepared to answer questions about which hotel you've chosen, why you chose it, and how much it will cost.

8. Scrambled up day! (Language Arts)
Write out 10 things that you did when you visited a city in the U.S.—it can be your hometown. Connect each sentence to the one before by using a transition word such as *dann* (then) or *nach* (after). Also repeat a bit of the sentence to make it clear which order the actions occurred in during the day. Cut the sentences up into strips and scramble them up. Give them to a partner and see how quickly he/she can put them into the correct sequence. Sentence examples: First we went to the movie theater in downtown Atlanta. After the movie theater, we went to the aquarium.

9. Why don't they use Fahrenheit over there? (Science, Math)
You want to go skiing in the Garmisch-Partenkirchen region over your Christmas break from school. You know it will be cold, but you need to check the weather and figure out how to plan for temperatures in Celsius. First, look up the weather in that region at that time of year. You can try this link: *http://de.weather.com/*. Then use this link to a conversion chart: *http://www.condoconcepts.com/convers.htm*. Figure out the average daytime and nighttime temperatures for the region you want to visit, in both Celsius and Fahrenheit.

10. Four corners (Physical Education, Social Studies)
Explain this game to students before you start. Label four corners (or areas) of the room with letters A, B, C, and D. You will read a question and give four possible choices for answers. The students are to pick the letter of the answer that best fits them and go to that corner of the room. Then they can discuss why they chose that corner. Use questions about travel. Here are five samples to get you started. Translate them into your language.

1. What German-speaking country would you most like to visit? (or Spanish speaking or French speaking)
   A. Germany B. Austria C. Switzerland D. Lichtenstein
2. What city would you most like to visit in southern Germany? (or southern France or southern Spain)
   A. Munich B. Stuttgart C. Heidelberg D. Regensburg
3. What method of public transportation would you most like to use to get around?
   A. bus B. subway C. streetcar D. car
4. What would you most need to pack to wear while in Germany in summer? (or France or Spain)
   A. shorts B. t-shirt C. pajamas D. jeans
5. What would you need on the plane trip to help time pass quickly?
   A. iPod B. a novel C. a Gameboy D. a magazine

Presentational Communicative Tasks

11. Visit My Hostel! (Art, Social Studies)
On a map of Germany, choose a small- to medium-sized town that you would like to visit and look it up in a book or online. Find out about the geography, weather, and special activities of the region. Create an ad for a youth hostel in or near this town. Include on the ad a picture showing the geographical elements of the region and information that any hostel would provide. This could include the owners, contact information, the number of beds/rooms, type of meals/dining rooms, price, people who can stay there, and activities available. Share your ad with the class and try to convince them to stay at your hostel. Make your hostel very appealing! Use this site if you need ideas about information to include: *http://www.jugendherberge.de/de/.*

12. My Future Trip (Social Studies, Art, Language Arts)
Research a German-speaking city that you would like to visit one day in the future. Create a PowerPoint about a two-week trip and include details such as what airlines you might take, where you might stay while there, what places you would be sure to visit, and what items you might look for to bring home with you. Present your PowerPoint to the class.
Teacher Note: Another format such as a poster may be used instead of Powerpoint.

13. Where will we stay? (Language Arts, Social Studies)
You and your family are planning to spend three weeks in Germany near Berlin. You want to rent a private home and you don't want to stay directly in the city. You decide to place an ad for a private home outside Berlin online. In your ad, include when you need the home, how much you will pay, what rooms you need, what transportation choices you want to have, and your contact information. Here is a website with ideas about how to write your ad in German: *http://www.allgrund.com/houses_for_rent_germany/how-to-rent-a-house-in-germany.html.*

14. I love my city! (Music, Social Studies)
Write a song about a German city that you love or would love to visit and include details about why the city is so great. Present your song to the class.

16. Come fly with me! (Language Arts, Social Studies)
You work at a travel agency and have been asked by a German family to prepare three different travel packages for them to look over to select a vacation. They want to see California and Nevada. Look online for three different airline/hotel package deals. Also find three or four sights/activities you could offer in each different travel package. For example, you might focus on sporting events for one package in case they are an athletic family. Then for another package you might focus on national parks in case they like to be outdoors. Alone or with a group of two or three others, create a presentation of the three choices and show it to the family.
Teacher Note: Choose people in the class to act as the family going on vacation. Tell students about websites such as orbitz.com *and* expedia.com *for travel packages and tips.*

Template K | Formative Assessment Task Template 1

Formative Speaking/Writing Task (select one)
Level __ - French/German/Spanish (select one)

Theme: (Select theme from local curriculum)
Topic: (Select topic from local curriculum)
Textbook Correlation: ______________

Task Objective:
To... (Try to keep this short. For example: To talk about a camping trip)

Task Description:
You are ... (Create a scenario. At the end of the task description, put in bold the main thing the student is to do.)

Minimum Requirements to Meet Expectations:
(Include..., Write...) (Try to list no more than 3–5 bullets)

Suggestions:
You may want to ... (Add additional ideas. Be careful not to suggest something they cannot do.)

Directions: You have ___ seconds to prepare and ___ seconds to speak. (speaking task)
You have ____ minutes to write a minimum of ______ sentences. (writing task)

Scoring Criteria: Level __ speaking/writing analytic rubric (chose one)

Say / Write (chose one) **as much as you can! Show off what you can do!**
(You may want to include here a graphic organizer for students to use when doing the task.)

Optional:

Teacher Note(s)
(Suggestions for teachers on what to introduce to students beforehand, what visuals to provide, etc.)

Template L
Formative Assessment Task Template 2

Formative Interactive Task

Level 3/Upper Level (choose one)

Program of Studies (POS) Theme: (POS theme)
POS Topic: (POS topic)
Textbook Correlation: ________

Task Objective:
To discuss . . . (Try to keep this short. For example: To discuss your vacation plans.)

Task Description:
(Create a scenario. At the end of the task description, put in bold the main thing the student is to do.)

Minimum Requirements to Meet Expectations:
(Try to list no more than 3–5 bullets)

Suggestions:

(Add additional ideas. For example:

You may want to ask your partner questions to help him/her elaborate.
You may want to mention . . .)

Directions: You have ___ **minutes** to read the task and to prepare separately what you are going to say.
You have ___ **minutes** for both partners to speak.

Scoring Criteria: Level ___ speaking/writing analytic rubric (choose one)

Say/Write (choose one) **as much as you can! Show off what you can do!**
(You may want to include here a graphic organizer for students to use when doing the task.)

Optional:
Teacher Note(s)
(Suggestions for teachers on what to introduce to students beforehand, what visuals to provide, etc.)

Template M
Sample Formative Assessment Task

Writing Task
Level 1 - French

Theme: Personal and Family Life

Topic: Clothing and Colors
Weather and Seasons; Interests and Leisure Activities

Task Objective:
To describe weather, seasons, and related clothing and activities

Task Description:
Your friend is coming to visit you in the winter. Your friend wants to know what the weather is like in the United States and what you wear. He/she also wants to know what you do for fun. Write your friend a letter about the weather, appropriate clothing, and likely activities for February.

Minimum Requirements to Meet Expectations:

- Describe what the weather is like.
- Describe at least three clothing items to bring.
- Describe at least three activities you do.

Suggestions:
You may want to ask your friend what he/she does in February.

Directions: You have 30 minutes to write a minimum of 10 sentences.

Scoring Criteria: Level 1 writing analytic rubric

Write as much as you can! Show off what you can do!

Weather	Clothing	Activities

Template N | Sample Integrated Performance Assessment (IPA)

Thematically Organized Assessment (TOA)
French

TOA Title: Il fait chaud! J'ai soif!

Theme: Art of Well-Being

Level: Novice-Mid

TOA Overview:
You and your friend are at your home and it's a hot summer day; you are very thirsty. The two of you decide you want something refreshing to drink. You decide to look up French beverage recipes on the Internet. After you select two recipes, you talk about the weather, how thirsty you are, which beverage you would like to drink, and why. You choose one of the recipes you found and show your friend the ingredients, how to make the beverage, and tell him/her why you like it.

Task Title: Il fait chaud! J'ai soif!

Theme: Art of Well-Being

Level: Novice-Mid **Focus Age Group:** Ages 10–12

National Standards Goals: Communication Communities

Communicative Mode: Interpretive

Time Frame: One 30-minute class period

Description of Task:
You and your friend are at your home and it's a hot summer day; you are very thirsty. Both of you decide you want something refreshing to drink. You look up recipes on the Internet.

Materials Needed: Copies of attached comprehension guide.

Teacher Notes:
1. Describe the task to the students (see description above).
2. Explain the rubric (see attached).
3. Distribute comprehension guide (see attached).
4. Students complete comprehension guide.

Please Note:
For original source of recipes, see website: http://www.recettes.qc.ca. Underneath the "Recettes" column, click on "Boissons." Select the following recipes:

Lait frappé

Limonade d'été

Nom____ Comprehension Guide

Il fait chaud! J'ai soif!

You and your friend are at your home and it's a hot summer day; you are very thirsty. Both of you decide you want something different to drink. You look up recipes on the Internet.

Recettes du Québec http://www.recettes.qc.ca	**Recettes du Québec** http://www.recettes.qc.ca
Lait frappé	**Limonade d'été**
Préparation: 15 minutes Cuisson: 0 minutes Portions: 1	Préparation: 5 minutes Cuisson: 0 minutes Portions: 1
Ingrédients	**Ingrédients**
3/4 de tasse ou 2 grosses boules de crème glacé 1/2 tasse de lait 1/4 cuillère à thé de vanille	1 à 1 1/2 jus de citron 1 tasse d'eau froide 1 cuillère à thé de sucre (au goût)
Méthode	**Méthode**
1. Mélanger tous les ingrédients dans un mélangeur ou directement dans un grand verre!	1. Mélanger le jus de citron, le sucre et l'eau. Servir froid.
Variante : Remplacer la crème glacé à la vanille par une saveur de votre choix (fraise, chocolat).	Recette envoyée par : Bernard

Circle the words that are mentioned in the two recipes.

First Recipe: Lait frappé

Milk Small Chocolate Vanilla Ingredients Ice cream

Milkshake Mix Big Banana Glass Ice

Second Recipe: Limonade d'été

Lemonade Cup Lime Cold Lemon Sugar

Orange Mix Hot Water Milk Juice

What are the names of these two drinks? ________________________________

What do you think is the difference between "Préparation" and "Cuisson"?

____

____

Novice-Mid Interpretive Rubric

Il fait chaud! J'ai soif!

	Exceeds Expectations	Meets Expectations	Does Not Meet Expectations
Can I understand what I read? (Comprehension)	I answer questions 1, 2, and 3 accurately.	I answer most of the questions 1, 2, and 3 accurately.	I answer questions 1, 2, and 3 inaccurately.
Can I understand the vocabulary? (Word Recognition)	I understand all the vocabulary in question 1.	I understand most of the vocabulary in question 1.	I understand only some of the vocabulary in question 1.
Can I identify the main idea? (Main Idea)	I identify the names of both of the recipes.	I identify the name of one of the recipes.	I do not identify the names of the recipes.
Do I infer meaning? (Interpretation)	I give the difference in meaning between "préparation" and "cuisson" in question #3.	I try to give the difference in meaning between "préparation" and "cuisson" in question #3.	I do not give the difference in meaning between "préparation" and "cuisson" in question #3.

Task Title: Il fait chaud! J'ai soif!

Theme: Art of Well-Being

Level: Novice-Mid **Focus Age Group:** Ages 10–12

National Standards Goals: Communication Connections Communities

Communicative Mode: Interpersonal

Time Frame: Depending on the number of students, one may need one or two 30-minute classes.

Description of Task:
You and your friend are at your home and it's a hot summer day. You talk about the following:

1. Weather
2. Thirst
3. Preference for milkshake or lemonade
4. Reason for preference

Materials Needed: None

Teacher Notes:
During prior lessons, students will have learned to talk about the weather and whether or not someone is thirsty.

1. Describe the task to the students (see description above).
2. Explain the rubric (see below).
3. Using a puppet, teacher models a possible dialogue.
4. Teacher should pair students with partners of similar ability.
5. Students talk with partners.
6. Teacher evaluates using scoring rubric.

Novice-Mid Interpretive Rubric

Il fait chaud! J'ai soif!

	Exceeds Expectations	Meets Expectations	Does Not Meet Expectations
Does the teacher understand me? (Comprehensibility)	My teacher understands me without difficulty.	My teacher understands me with occasional difficulty.	My teacher understands me with much difficulty.
Do I understand my partner? (Comprehension)	I understand my partner without difficulty.	I understand my partner but sometimes need repetition or restatement.	Most of the time I don't understand my partner.
How well do I use the French language? (Vocabulary Use & Language Control)	I am mostly correct when producing simple sentences. I am mostly correct when attempting to create sentences. I recognize and use vocabulary with ease.	I am somewhat correct with memorized language. I am less correct when attempting to create sentences. I recognize and use most of the vocabulary correctly.	I am accurate only at the word level. I have limited use of words / phrases.
How well do I keep the conversation going? (Communication Strategies)	I begin to recombine some memorized language to keep the conversation going. I ask for repetition and/ or clarification.	I use memorized chunks of language to keep the conversation going. I ask for repetition. I tell my partner when I do not understand.	I do not demonstrate an ability to keep the conversation going.

Task Title: Il fait chaud! J'ai soif!

Theme: Art of Well-Being

Level: Novice-Mid **Focus Age Group:** Ages 10–12

National Standards Goals: Communication Culture Connections

Communicative Mode: Presentational

Time Frame: Depending on the number of students, one may need one or two 30-minute classes.

Description of Task:
It's a very hot summer day and you decide to make yourself something cold to drink. Choose one of the two recipes, milkshake or lemonade, and show your friends how to make it.

- Choose one of the two recipes, milkshake or lemonade.
- Show and state all the necessary ingredients.
- Tell what to do with the ingredients.
- Drink your beverage.
- State why you like it.
- Use culturally appropriate gesture to indicate delicious recipe.

If you prefer, you can create a different cold drink and show your friends how it's made.

Materials Needed:
Teacher will need to supply either real or toy foods for the following recipes

1. Milkshake recipe
   a. Ice cream
   b. Milk
   c. Vanilla
   d. Glass
   e. Ice-cream scoop
   f. Teaspoon
   g. Measuring cup

2. Lemonade
   a. Lemon juice
   b. Water
   c. Sugar
   d. Glass
   e. Teaspoon

Teacher Notes:
Describe the task to the students (see description above).

1. Explain the rubric. 2. Students prepare. 3. Students present.

Novice-Mid Interpretive Rubric

Il fait chaud! J'ai soif!

	Exceeds Expectations	Meets Expectations	Does Not Meet Expectations
Can the audience understand me? (Comprehensibility)	The audience understands me without difficulty even though I may have some hesitation when I speak.	The audience generally understands me. I may have some hesitations or unnatural pauses when I speak.	I am not clearly understood. I have frequent hesitations and many unnatural pauses.
How well do I use the French language? (Language Control & Vocabulary Use)	I am correct with memorized language but as I begin to create (produce simple sentences) with the language, I have difficulty being correct. My presentation is rich in appropriate vocabulary.	I am mostly correct with memorized language. I accurately use vocabulary that I have been taught.	I am correct only at the word level. My vocabulary is limited and/or repetitive.
How well do I capture and maintain the audience's attention? (Impact)	I use gestures, visuals, and tone of voice to maintain my audience's attention.	I use some gestures and visuals to maintain my audience's attention.	I make no effort to maintain my audience's attention.
How well do I organize the presentation? (Communication Strategies)	My presentation has a beginning, middle, and an end. My main ideas are supported with examples.	My presentation has a beginning, middle, and an end.	I present information randomly.
How well would I pass for a native speaker? (Cultural Awareness)	I demonstrate some awareness of cultural appropriateness. • Appropriate use of formal vs. informal language. • Use of language-specific "fillers." • Use of gestures.	I occasionally use a culturally appropriate gesture and sometimes use appropriate register (formal vs. informal)	I do not use any culturally appropriate language or gestures.

Template O | Sample Integrated Performance Assessment (IPA)

Thematically Organized Assessment (TOA)
Spanish

TOA Title: Una Casa en España

Theme: What Makes My House A Home

Level: Intermediate-Low

TOA Overview:
What an experience! Your family is moving to Spain for a year. Your mother will be working on a special project for her company and everyone will spend the year abroad. A packet of information for the move arrives in the mail. Your mother is confused by some of the documents and asks you to help her interpret the information because you have been learning Spanish since elementary school.

One of her first concerns is housing. You scan online real estate ads to find appropriate places to live. After talking over the options with your family, you speak by telephone with a real estate agent in Spain to discuss the lodgings that interest your family and to find out additional details about the layout, rooms, furniture, and amenities.

Your family bought a home in Barcelona and everyone is looking forward to the experience of living abroad. Once you arrive in the country, you help your parents communicate ideas to the decorator. You write a detailed description of your family's likes and dislikes, the amenities you need and want, and make suggestions about furniture and accessories for the house. You even draw a layout of the house and label the items you want in each room.

Task Title: Una Casa en España

Theme: What Makes My House A Home.

Level: Intermediate-Low **Focus Age Group:** 13+

National Standards Goals: Communication Cultures

Communicative Mode: Interpretive

Time frame: One class period (40 minutes)

Description of Task:
After searching the Internet for real estate ads for houses and apartments to rent or buy in Spain, you find a few places that look interesting. In order to present the information to your family, you scan the ads carefully and jot down important information.

Materials Needed: Websites and Interpretive Task sheets

http://www.jekoo.com/search.asp?cln=oldrkeov&mkt=es&typ=jekoo_1&src=0&adv=1&key=Inmobiliaria+espana&ksc=Inmobiliaria+espana

http://www.spainhouses.net/es/index.php

http://www.fotocasa.es/index.aspx

http://www.jerezinmobiliaria.com/casas1.htm

Teacher Notes:
Scan the websites listed above to find appropriate real estate ads for the task. Choose at least three to five homes that students might use to complete the Comprehension Guide. You might print out ads or allow students to search online.

Interpretive Activity Sheet
Una Casa en España

I. After scanning the ads, you organize the information about the houses and apartments by filling in a chart about each residence.

Name/Number of Residence	Type of Residence	Location	Size	Rooms	Special Features

II. Compare your residence to one of the Spanish residences:

____

____

____

III. Some of the words were unfamiliar. You made guesses about the meanings.

1. inmobiliaria______________________________
2. particulares ______________________________
3. en alquiler ______________________________
4. piso ______________________________
5. planta baja______________________________

IV. Answer the following questions by providing as many reasons as you can. Your responses may be in English.

1. Which house/apartment do you prefer and why?
   Use details from the ads to support your answers.

____

____

____

____

2. So you believe that your family will enjoy their stay in Spain?
   Explain.

____

____

____

____

Intermediate-Interpretive Rubric

Una Casa en España

	Exceeds Expectations	**Meets Expectations**	**Does Not Meet Expectations**
Can I identify the main idea? (Main Idea)	I identify the main ideas presented in text.	I identify the main ideas of the text.	I do not identify the main ideas of the text.
Can I understand supporting details? (Comprehension)	I understand most supporting details of the text.	I understand some supporting details.	I understand few supporting details.
Can I infer meaning? (Interpretation)	I infer the meaning of most cognates and word families. I derive the meaning of a few new words from context. I infer the author's intent. My answers demonstrate some cultural awareness.	I infer the meaning of some cognates and word families. I do not derive the meaning of new words from context. My answers demonstrate little cultural awareness.	I infer the meaning of few cognates and word families. I do not derive the meaning of new words from context. My answers do not demonstrate cultural awareness.

Task Title: Una Casa en España

Theme: What Makes My House A Home

Level: Intermediate-Low **Focus Age Group:** 13+

National Standards Goals: Communication Comparison

Communicative Mode: Interpersonal

Time Frame: 40 minutes

Description of Task:
Your mother asks you to speak with a real estate agent in Spain concerning housing for your family. You place the call and have a conversation about possible locations, the advantages of renting or buying a place, whether to look for an apartment or a house, and the rooms and amenities your family requires. Before ending the conversation, make sure you give the agent your address and phone number so that she might mail you ads and call with additional information.

Intermediate-Low Interpersonal Rubric

Una Casa en España

	Exceeds Expectations	Meets Expectations	Does Not Meet Expectations
How well do I communicate? (Text Type)	I create with the language by using strings of sentences.	I create with language by using simple sentences and some strings of sentences.	I use simple sentences, isolated words, and memorized phrases.
How well do I understand you? (Comprehension)	I am generally understood. My accuracy helps me get my point across.	I am generally understood. There are some errors, but they do not distort message.	I am understood with occasional difficulty.
What kind of vocabulary do I use? (Language Use & Vocabulary)	I use many words and expressions from different topics in the appropriate context most of the time. I provide some supporting details from my own life and the article.	I use a combination of words from different topics. Occasionally I may use the wrong word or expression.	I use basic and repetitive vocabulary and may resort to English when I am unable to communicate my message.
How well do I keep the conversation going? (Communication Strategies)	I ask and answer questions to maintain the conversation and to clarify. At times, I paraphrase to make myself understood.	I maintain a simple conversation by asking some questions and answering questions.	I respond to basic, direct questions and ask simple questions.

Task Title: Una Casa en España

Theme: What Makes My House A Home

Level: Intermediate-Low **Focus Age Group:** 13+

National Standards Goals: Communication Cultures Comparisons

Communicative Mode: Presentational

Time Frame: One class period (40 minutes)

Description of Task:
Your family has arrived in Spain. Your parents are meeting with a decorator and need your help once again. You write a detailed description of your family members' likes and dislikes, the furniture you want and need in each room, and make suggestions about furniture and accessories for the house. You even draw a layout of the house and label the items you want in each room.

Materials Needed: Drawing paper.

Intermediate-Low Presentational Rubric

Una casa en España

	Exceeds Expectations	Meets Expectations	Does Not Meet Expectations
How do I communicate? (Text Type)	I create with language using strings of sentences.	I create with language using simple sentences. I use some strings of sentences.	I use mostly simple sentences and memorized phrases with some attempts to create personal meaning.
How well am I understood? (Comprehensibility)	I am easily understood. I express my ideas clearly.	I am generally understood. I clearly express most of my ideas.	I am understood with occasional difficulty. I do not clearly express my ideas.
What kind of vocabulary do I use? (Language Use & Vocabulary)	I use a wide variety of vocabulary on several aspects of the topic with very little repetition.	I use some variety of vocabulary on a few aspects of the topic with some repetition.	I use basic and/or repetitive vocabulary most of the time.
How accurate is my language?	I am very accurate when producing simple sentences. My accuracy may decrease when I use more complex language.	I am generally accurate when producing simple sentences. I may be less accurate when adding details.	I am mostly accurate with memorized language. My accuracy may decrease a lot when trying to create with the language.
How well do I get the attention of my audience? (Impact)	I make good choices of phrases, images, and content to maintain the attention of the audience/ reader.	I make some good choices of phrases, images, and content to maintain the attention of the audience/ reader.	I use mostly gestures or visuals to maintain audience's attention. I use some phrases, but my vocabulary conveys very basic information.
How organized and smooth is my presentation? (Communication Strategies)	I organize my presentation in a logical manner. I speak/write with fluency.	I organize my presentation in a logical manner. I pause a few times, disrupting the flow.	I focus mostly on the completion of the task; I do not pay much attention to organization and flow of my presentation.
How well do I demonstrate cultural awareness? (Cultural Awareness)	I include information and ideas that reflect Spanish products and practices.	I include some information and ideas that reflect Spanish products and practices.	I demonstrate little or no knowledge of Spanish products and practices.

Template P
Sample Lesson Plan: Chinese

My Pets

Object: Students will be able to

- Identify 10 animals/pets correctly (e.g., 牛 – *cow,* 马 – *horse,* 羊 – *sheep,* 鸟 – *bird,* 狗 – *dog,* 猫 – *cat,* 鱼 – *fish,* 金鱼 – *goldfish,* 老鼠 – *mice,* 老虎 – *tiger*)
- Correctly state numbers of pets (两条金鱼, 一只狗, 一头牛)
- Exchange information about animals/pets (e.g., 你家有动物吗? Do you have any animals/pets? 你家有 . . . (狗)吗? or, 你家有没有 . . . (狗)? Do you have . . . ? How many . . . do you have? 你有几只/条 . . .)
- State which one of Chinese zodiac animals they are
- Understand similarities and differences between pet-keeping in China and in their own culture

Standard: 1.1: Interpersonal Communication
1.2: Perspectives and Practices of the Culture
4.2: Cultural Comparisons

Procedures:

1. Warm up: Get acquainted with students, telling my name and asking both their English and Chinese name as well as their age.
2. Hook: Chinese zodiac animals
3. Presentation: Using PowerPoint to present the new vocabulary—names of animals and measure words and adjective words that describe certain qualities of animals.

Practice: What are you going to do?

1. Present animals words with measure words and have students repeat, as a class and individually, to practice pronunciation.
2. Ask students if they have any of these animals as pets using the patterns: 你家有 . . . (狗)吗？ or, 你家有没有 . . . （狗）？Then, ask them how many (animals) do they have? 你有几只/条 . . . ？ In between, recycle both patterns using third person pronouns: 他ta, 她ta: 他/她家有... (狗)吗？ 他/她家有几只/条 . . . (狗)？ What kind of animal(s) does s/he have? How many?
3. Show a Chinese Zodiac Animal table mat from Chinese restaurants and ask students which animal year they were born and what are their family members' animals: 你属什么？
4. Give students a sheet of paper to interview at least three classmates using vocabulary and patterns, and then randomly call on each student to report them.
5. Show a picture of a cute puppy in Beijing. Have students compare similarities and differences of pet-keeping culture in China and their own country with words and patterns they have, such as: 很喜欢，爱，有，etc.

Closure:

Go over animal words and sentences orally; then pass out a hand-out: Match pictures with Chinese words.

Template Q
Thank You Letter

High School

[date]

Mr. John Doe
1000 Any Street
Any Town, State Zip

Dear Mr. Doe,

I want to thank you so much for providing bagels for our teachers at our Foreign Language staff development program on [date]. Refreshments are such an important part of any conference or in-service. Once the teachers had enjoyed the breakfast, they were invigorated and ready to begin the morning session. Thank you so much for thinking of us, as usual.

Let me also thank you, on behalf of the teachers, for the excellent support we always received from the PTA.

As the Spanish teacher at Mountain View H.S., I look forward to working with you throughout the school year.

Sincerely,

Sally McBride
Foreign Language Coordinator

Template R
Teacher Recommendation

[date]

To whom it may concern:

It is with great pleasure that I am able to recommend Alison Angel. Alison is a dynamic and intelligent high school junior at Mountain View High School. Last year I had the pleasure of having this extremely gifted student in my Spanish 3 class and this year she is continuing with the AP Spanish Language course. Alison enjoys learning and taking challenges. She represents the best of what an American high school student can be: motivated enough to set high standards and hard working enough to achieve those lofty goals.

In Spanish, and I am sure it is the same in her other classes, she has never had an unexcused tardy or absence. Rather she arrives first to class and is always prepared to learn. Dedicated to her studies, Alison thrives in a challenging and scholarly environment. She never turns in a late or incomplete assignment. In fact, Alison expects the most from herself and maintains a 4.0 in Spanish. Although Alison carries the highest grade of any student I teach, she readily completes any extra credit assignment I assign. She simply wants to perfect her language skills on a continual basis. She has always had the curiosity and the drive to search for a challenging opportunity to enrich her proficiency in a subject area. I have no doubt that Alison Angel is the best candidate to work with students over the summer, especially in the area of Spanish.

Alison consistently selects and succeeds at Mountain View's toughest courses. She is able to balance her academics with her extracurricular activities. She is in the Spanish Honor Society and the National Honor Society and has won numerous academic honors.

Alison's hard work and dedication are true character traits, which separate her from many other students I have taught. When any student in the class does not understand a concept, she does not hesitate to help him or her. She is a silent leader and is admired by her peers. Through her persistence, she has developed into an excellent Spanish student striving for more.

Alison Angel is quite simply a wonderfully talented young woman with a strong intellect and exemplary personal values, who will be a tremendous asset wherever she goes. She is a role model for peers and adults alike and is accorded a great deal of respect by all of those who come in contact with her. It is with the highest degree of confidence and enthusiasm that I recommend her!

Sincerely,

Jeff Baxter
Spanish Instructor

Template S | Recommendation for Student

[date]

To whom it may concern:

I am pleased to recommend Steven Fischer. Steven was a student in my German II, III, and IV classes. I have since transferred to another school, but understand that Steven still plans to be very active in all German activities.

In my association with Steven, I have been extremely impressed with him. Steven is an enthusiastic student and a sincere, hard-working young man, possessed of intellectual maturity and a dedication to excellence in his education. He is self-motivated and well-organized. I feel he has insight, is a creative thinker and is an excellent prospect for your institution. Steven always did an excellent job of balancing a strong academic program with many extracurricular activities. He has always taken a full range of advanced classes, was a member of the school football, basketball, and soccer teams, and participated in many local competitions.

German did not come easily for Steven. I was told this early in his freshman year and was amazed because Steven's hard-work and dedication more than made up for this fact. He always asked intelligent questions and never allowed himself to get behind if he did not understand a concept. In short, he never gives up!

Steven's pleasant personality and his dedication to excellence are welcome examples for all students to follow. I enthusiastically recommend Steven for admission to your institution. I am confident that he will grow and contribute much wherever he goes.

Sincerely,

Jakob Mann
German Instructor

Template T Invitation to School Event

Dear Parents:

The Foreign Language Department will host the second annual International Night on [date] at [time]. The students and faculty wish to extend an invitation to you and your family to join in the festivities. Enclosed you will find a pass to admit you and your family to the concert following the open house as well as a schedule so that you can plan your evening.

We know you will enjoy the event. The students would also welcome your attendance at the presentation of awards shortly after the concert to acknowledge the students' hard work and achievements this event represents.

We look forward to seeing you on [date]. If you have any questions or need additional information, please call ____________ at ________________.

Sincerely,

[Teacher]
[School]

Template U
Back-To-School Information for Parents

Mountain View High School
Back-to-School Night

Spanish 1, 2, & 3
[date]

Success in foreign language requires self discipline. New concepts build on concepts that were previously taught. Therefore, students need to do assigned work on a daily basis. Parents frequently ask teachers, "What can I do to help my son or daughter in learning a foreign language?" The following information is provided in response to that question.

Objectives

1. To actively involve parents in the education of their child
2. To provide parents with information that will enable them to contribute to the progress of their child in foreign language study

Each student should have the following materials:

1. 3-ring binder, textbook, and workbook
2. Pencils, pens, highlighter
3. Planner or assignment calendar from the teacher

Things a parent can do on a daily basis:

1. Provide a quiet comfortable study area at home.
2. Check your student's assignment sheet/planner for homework, quizzes, and tests. Students and parents can always get assignments by logging on to my web page http.//www.__________ or http.//www.schoolnotes.com.
3. When checking assignments look for the following:
   a. Is the assignment complete?
   b. Did your son or daughter refer to his/her notes for examples of the assigned work?
   c. If your child says he/she did not understand the sentence or question, did he or she consult the vocabulary section in the back of the textbook?
   d. After studying for a quiz or test, did your child make a practice quiz in order to test himself?
   e. It is helpful to use a cassette recorder to practice vocabulary and pronunciation.
4. Remind your child that simply looking at words does not mean he/she has memorized them. Students must always write them down and use them in context, then read the sentences aloud. This technique will guarantee better results with long-term memory.

If your son or daughter is absent from school:

1. If your child is absent, please have him/her check my web page for the homework assignment or contact his/her homework buddy.
2. Please remind your son or daughter to make up homework, classwork, quizzes, and tests as soon as possible upon returning to school.
3. Please remind your child to ask the teacher for the assignments if there is a prearranged absence.

Extra help is available:

I am in my room after school on Tuesdays and Thursdays to help students. If your child prefers peer tutoring, I can make arrangements to have an honor society student there to help him/her if it is prearranged. Have your child discuss this with me.

A weekly progress report, for all classes, is available upon request. I send out interim reports to all students.

- Interim reports will be issued on the following dates. Please record the dates below on your calendar.
  [list dates]
- Please call or e-mail me if there is a problem. My e-mail address is: mary.marvelous@mtview.edu . Under subject, please write your child's full name. If I do not recognize your e-mail address, I may delete it by mistake.

Please note:

1. If you would like to have me send you feedback on your child's progress, please e-mail me at any time. Because I am teaching during the day, please allow at least 24 hours for me to respond.
2. If you do not have access to a computer, please call me during the day [time] at [phone number]. I can also provide a computer printout of your child's grades on a regular basis, but this should be arranged in advance.

For additional information, contact:

Mary Marvelous
Mountain View High School
Phone: [phone number]

Chapter 3
Difficult Moments

Everyone has moments when things do not seem to work out as planned. Teachers are no exception. You can't prevent these moments from occurring, but you can do some things now that will prepare you to deal with surprises when they occur. A veteran teacher once had a central office supervisor come for an unannounced observation. It was on the day of her school's International Fair. The teacher was surprised to see the supervisor waiting at her door at 7:15 a.m., but felt she had a good lesson planned and could carry on without undue stress.

Suddenly she remembered that she had told her students to bring the bratwursts to her room first thing in the morning and she would keep them on ice until the fair started. As students often do, many forgot to bring them before first period started so had to get a pass out of homeroom to deliver them to her. During the first 40 minutes of her lesson, a stream of students came by her room with bratwursts in hand. Without skipping a beat, the teacher glided to the door to receive bratwursts, while pointing to a picture on the overhead with one hand and placing brats in the cooler with the other. She recalled the episode as her "Bratwurst Ballet."

As it turned out, the observer was fascinated that the teacher did not let the interruptions derail her lesson and was truly impressed at the control and self-confidence the teacher displayed. The episode would have sent many teachers into a tailspin, but this teacher made it look like an everyday occurrence. Her calm demeanor kept the class on task and allowed instruction to continue. Later, she confessed she was dying on the inside, but not about to let it show.

This chapter will give you some tried and true ideas about preparing for the unexpected. Every teacher needs to have backup plans in their kit bag. Experienced teachers usually do, because they have faced wacky situations in their careers at one time or another. As a first-year teacher, you are most at jeopardy when mishaps occur unexpectedly to derail your classroom plan. Being caught off-guard slows down the problem-solving process, adding to your duress. This chapter will give you examples of what kinds of emergencies could happen in your classroom—and provide time-tested solutions that can at least limit your grief when a mishap occurs.

Mid-Lesson Changes

Every teacher has to admit that now and then, a lesson plan bombs. You could be in the middle of what you thought was a wonderful lesson and notice that not one student is paying attention. Your students appear to be clueless about what you are imparting to them. What do you do? Here are your choices:

- Continue on as if nothing is going wrong. You spent hours last night writing this lesson and you will see it through to the end.
- Change activities but keep the focus on the same topic and see if you can re-engage the students.
- Stop and ask the students for feedback. Check to see:

- if they are confused about the content or objectives.
- if they understand what the purpose for the lesson is. Did you take time to explain how this lesson fits into the big picture?
- if they have experienced "information overload" and need time to digest the material.
- if they need more time to practice what they have learned.
- if your expectations are too high or too low.
- if they understand where you are going with the lesson.

Usually a few questions will give you the information you need to proceed. Once you have identified the cause of the lesson malfunction, back up, and regroup. Be prepared to go back and explain things again. Always have a Plan B. The following tips will help you develop a "Plan B":

- Divide the class into groups and assign each group a different topic to research and "teach" on the subject you wanted to cover. When students have to teach vocabulary, a cultural point, demonstrate the use of vocabulary in a dialogue or skit, then you turn passive learning into active learning and involve students in reaching the desired outcomes.
- Have a folder of pictures that can be used for any topic. Use the pictures to elicit conversation, to write a dialogue, to write a journal entry, to create a story, or to describe family members, clothing, weather, activities—which involves students in your lesson. The objectives of the lesson can remain the same. You are only changing the strategies to involve the students and give them more opportunities to use the concepts you are teaching.
- Have two teams of students reach into a hat and pull out a scenario. Each team is to act out the scenario described on the card. The students vote on the best "improv" and the team with the most votes gets a certificate. After 10 or 15 minutes, you will likely find your students focused and ready for another activity.
- If you find your expectations for this lesson were too high, shift gears and give the students an opportunity to master smaller units before proceeding. This will also give the students more confidence along the way. You can revise your lesson plan and continue it the next time you meet the class, and you'll probably find students participating to a greater degree because they now have a better grasp of the basics.
- If students seem "lost," form small groups and have them discuss the major concepts that have been taught, jot them down on a piece of newsprint, and have a member of each group report its thoughts on the subject. Group discussions help students who did miss some portions of the lesson to "catch up."

It's always OK to be honest with students and admit that perhaps your lesson was a bit ambitious. Students will appreciate your sensitivity about stopping to reteach or reorganize. Students are savvy. If they sense that you want to get from A to Z whether or not all your students are keeping up, they may give up and tune out. Always read your students' body language and ask frequent questions to be constantly aware of how your lesson is going. Also be prepared to have a very successful lesson from one year off track the very next year. Students are different. So when you plan lessons always take into account the makeup of your class—and have a back-up plan at all times.

Student Confrontation

At some point in time during your career, you will encounter a student confrontation in one form or another. Nine times out of 10, it has less to do with you and more to do with what happened 10 minutes before class—a family situation, a break-up, a need to be the "attention getter" in the class, or a combination of all the above. Students in the class are more affected by how you react than by the student's actions. Keep in mind that the confrontational student wants you to react. If you put yourself at his or her level you will lose the respect of the other students. It takes strength to remain calm and defuse the situation, but that will resolve the situation in most cases. Reprimanding students in front of their peers leaves them no way out of the contretemps. It is important for students to save face in front of their peers.

You will exacerbate the situation if you demand an apology or argue with the student in front of the class. That can cost you the respect of your students, not to mention valuable class time. So to defuse a student confrontation, use techniques like these:

- In a quiet, matter-of-fact tone, say, "I know you are upset. Have a seat and we will discuss this after class."
- You may also validate what the student is trying to say by telling him, "I hear what you are saying. Let's discuss this further after class."
- Say, "I think you need some space. Would you like to stand outside the classroom for a few minutes and come back in

when you have calmed down?" This gives the student an out without having to win or lose the argument. When you are aware that the student has calmed down, you can hand him a note suggesting he stay after class to talk with you.

- Place a chair right outside the classroom, where you can see it, give the student a legal pad and ask him sit and write down what it is that is bothering him, and re-enter the classroom quietly when he is finished. Now you'll have his talking points if you need to set up a meeting after class or after school.
- If you feel the student is a danger to you or the other students, call the office or send a reliable student to the office to summon assistance from an administrator. Never send an upset student to the office alone.
- Do not let yourself be drawn into an argument. Remember to keep your voice calm and be in control of the situation.

When you have an opportunity to talk to a confrontational student one-on-one, you may or may not learn what triggered the outburst. But explain that in no circumstance are his or her actions acceptable, and that if it happens again you will have to call home or report it to the office. Then come up with a plan. Many schools support a contract between the teacher and the students that outlines expectations and requires monitoring and reporting regularly to parents. Your guidance counseling staff also should be able to assist with this process if necessary.

If the student should feel too upset in the near future to continue in class, that could be a signal to send (or accompany) the student to the guidance office, or clinic for "time out."

If you can find out the cause of the problem and work on a solution, most likely the student will not only appreciate your concern, but may even feel you are someone she can trust and confide in. However, there are times when a guidance counselor would be the best next step. You will not be able to solve all problems that easily, but at least you can be a facilitator in turning a bad situation around and a model for your students in how it is done.

Technology Malfunctions

Always be prepared for technology to fail. Having a movie planned and discovering at the start of class that the VCR or DVD player will not work can be a painful experience. Similarly, discovering your classroom computer is not operational after you worked all night on a PowerPoint presentation will only lead to frustration if you are not well provisioned. At times like these, how do you occupy your students for the next 90 minutes? Here's a check-off list for dealing with technology malfunctions:

- Be sure you have an extra bulb for your overhead projector on hand.
- Make transparencies of your PowerPoint presentation so that you can use the overhead if the computer doesn't work.
- Post a copy of your presentation in case the overhead projector doesn't work.
- Save any electronic file on the school server or on a flash drive. That way, if you have it saved on a CD and the server crashes, you will be prepared.
- Keep an extension cord in your desk in case a wall outlet is dead.
- Test your video/DVD the day before you plan to show it.
- If you use cassette recorders in class for performance assessments, check batteries and headsets the day before administering the assessments.
- If you use laptops with your students, make sure they have CD drives if the lesson requires the use of CDs.
- Be sure ahead of time that all computers in the lab are working. If you have fewer computers than students, decide in advance which students will work together on one computer.
- Check the light in the LCD projector and the cords connecting it to the computer.
- If your language requires software to create symbols and characters, make sure all computers in the lab have the software loaded and are ready to be switched over to the target language. And at every PC have instructions on how to type using its characters/symbols.
- In case the server in your district or at your school crashes, have an emergency lesson handy.
- Always have a flash drive with you (preferably with 1 GB of memory) in case the server goes down in a lab situation. Students will be able to save their work to the desktop and you can go around and save each document to the flash drive.
- Know where a second CD player is located in case the one in your classroom fails.
- Have extra CDs and cassette tapes in case a student needs one.

Those are just some of the ways you can survive technology malfunctions. Probably most important is to get to know the technology experts in your school. They can be life-savers when tech quirks pop up. But don't neglect to have back-up lessons at the ready, because even the tech folks get bogged down at times.

The Unexpected Parent Visit

In most cases, if parents want to schedule a conference with you, they know to contact you in advance to set it up. After all, that information is in the kit you distributed at the beginning of the year. It is also a good idea to have the student's guidance counselor involved in the conference.

There are times when parents want to hold an impromptu conference, with little or no notice—when they drop in without notice between classes or after school, or want special time at Back-to-School Night or an after-school function. If a parent comes to your classroom unannounced to talk to you, explain that you will be happy to have a conference, but to be fair to the student, it is best to schedule the conference when there would be enough time to discuss the situation fully. You are not obligated to talk to a parent between classes or at any unannounced time. Explain to a drop-in parent that you need time to prepare for a conference and coordinate it with the counselor so that the outcome will benefit the student.

If a drop-in parent is simply upset about the student's grade, you may tell the parent you'll call after school or in the evening to discuss the grade. In a phone call, if the parent becomes belligerent, explain politely that you will have to end the call and ask the parent to schedule a conference at a time convenient for both of you. If that doesn't suit the parent, ask if you can reply by e-mail. This will give the parent time to calm down and allow you time to prepare a response. If the dialogue goes beyond the issue of the student's grade, encourage the parent to come in for a conference.

The Difficult Parent Conference

Parents generally schedule parent/teacher conferences to find out how they can help their child. If you come well-prepared to the conference, the meeting usually ends on a good note. You and the parents develop a plan for their student and agree to communicate periodically on the student's performance.

There are times when parent conferences do not go as smoothly as you may wish. If you feel the parents are emotional about an issue or if you have already experienced a difficult phone conversation with them, be sure to include the counselor and even the assistant principal in the conference. Brief the counselor and assistant principal about the out-of-control phone conversation. Ask them if you may be excused from the conference should the parent again fly off the handle during the conference. It is up to you to explain your concerns to your administrators and make sure you have their support in the event the conference gets out of hand. Nobody wants to be blindsided in a conference. As long as you talk in a calm voice, are positive, and show honest concern for the student, your administrators should support and protect you.

Medical Emergencies

It is important to flag students in your grade book if they have any type of medical condition that may need special attention. The administration should give you a list of students in this category at the beginning of the year. If you do not get such a list, check with the school nurse to learn if any of your students are in this category.

You need information in order to react appropriately if the student should experience an allergic reaction to a bee sting, has food allergies, needs medication, or has another condition that may suddenly need your full attention. Make sure you are briefed about these students—how to spot episodes, what causes them, and how you should proceed to assist the student. For example, a teacher who did not know one of his students was diabetic sent her to the clinic alone when she complained of dizziness. On the way there, she passed out. Luckily, a teacher witnessed her collapse and immediately called for help. This critical situation could have been avoided if the teacher had helped the student to the clinic at the moment she experienced dizziness.

Student illnesses are confidential and you should protect the students' privacy by not discussing a student's medical condition with anyone unless you have the parents' permission or by checking with the school nurse. Some students are embarrassed about their condition and you should talk to the school nurse or counselor about how you should best handle a sensitive condition. Establish a routine with each such student in your class. For example, you can allow a student who will need to visit the restroom immediately to do so without taking time to ask permission. Students who have to go to the clinic to take regularly scheduled medication may need to arrive late to class or to have hall passes issued in advance. You might establish a signal for alerting you to an emergency situation, since time usually is an important factor in these cases.

It is more difficult to address classroom situations in which students who do not have special medical conditions need to alert you to a health emergency situation. For guidance on separating legitimate emergencies from not-so-urgent needs, many teachers use the following strategies:

- Issue each student three hall passes per quarter. Each unused hall pass can be redeemed at the end of the quarter for what you feel would be a special treat. This could include fun stickers, a free homework pass, an extra day on a project, or extra points. Let it be each student's decision to use a pass without explaining its use to the teacher. A student who uses a pass with a medical explanation to the teacher would be able to receive replacement passes.
- Have a sign-in sheet at the door for any student arriving late to class. If the student was in the clinic, she could indicate this on the sheet, which the teacher would later check against the clinic sign-in records.
- Have brightly colored "I just want you to know…" forms for students to fill out as necessary and present to you in class. Topics on these forms might include the following issues:
  - I do not feel well and may need to go to the clinic.
  - I am upset and may need to visit my counselor.
  - I need to talk to you when you get a chance.
  - I need to use the restroom as soon as possible.

This gives you time to consider your response and fill out any appropriate forms or passes without drawing undue attention to a problem the student is experiencing. It should be understood that the nurse, counselor, or office personnel will sign your form when the student reaches the desired destination, and that it will be returned to you when the student is back in the classroom. This provides you with a record of the student's whereabouts when not in your classroom.

Interruptions

It is difficult sometimes to get through a week without an interruption of some sort. Interruptions seem to come at the most inopportune times. You may be the most organized teacher, with lesson plans outlining every minute of a class period, but when the fire alarm sounds or an emergency assembly is announced, flexibility is the name of the game. You sometimes need to make quick decisions about which activities in your lesson can be cut, to allow you to achieve your objectives for that lesson.

There are times when you may lose the entire class period because of a storm or other community calamity. It is important to remember that the students should not be the ones to bear the brunt of the interruption to instruction. It is better to adjust the other classes (that are following the same lesson plan) than to expect the students from the class that experienced the interruption to do extra work.

Some teachers think they have to hurry and catch the one class up to the others, but in reality, all students can benefit from review and practice. Decide how you can give those classes time to practice what they have learned, while giving the students who missed one day the time to learn the material. Teachers in areas that experience "snow days" and "late openings" are usually the most experienced in flexibility. Some winters create scenarios where a teacher may see only second period classes five days in a month. If you think this might happen to you, it's best to prepare students with an emergency packet that includes the following:

- Website links for practice.
- Instructions on what students should do if out of school for a number of days.
- Established routines so that students know which textbooks are to be taken home on a daily basis during times when schools are closed (because of severe weather, for instance).
- Instructions for completing workbook pages, textbook lessons, CD practice, Blackboard (or another course management system) instruction, and worksheets for practice.
- Projects and research that can be completed at home when schools are closed.
- Reminders that students can call a homework buddy from class so that oral communication drills can be completed while at home.
- A check-off sheet you've developed that students can use to show what work was completed during the emergency.

These ideas have come from many teachers in the Snow Belt, but if you teach in an area that experiences storms of any kind, it is best to be prepared and to have your students prepared. Many districts are also having teachers prepare for the possibility of a pandemic.

Difficult Responses

In Chapter 2, communication with parents was discussed. From time to time you will receive a difficult e-mail or letter from a parent. Writing the proper response is critical. It should go without saying that you shouldn't answer when you are angry. Put the message aside for the moment. Take some time to think about your response. Write a first draft. Think about how you can take the emotion out of the response in order to defuse the situation. Most important, avoid sarcasm in your response.

Keep these basic principles in mind when writing your final draft:

- Focus on basic good writing techniques.
- Be prompt. You do not want to inflame a situation by not addressing the concern in a timely fashion.
- Be careful. Answering criticism can be a delicate matter, even when there is no real foundation for the critic's concern or complaint.
- Neutralize the complaint.
- Answer all concerns and criticisms rationally. Don't try to win a verbal battle.
- Remember that every letter makes some sort of impression on the reader, and in a sense every letter is an instrument of public relations. Expect your letter to be circulated among other parents.
- Follow this order: Think, write, rewrite, and look again.
- Have someone else read your response before sending it. This will be required in many schools.
- Be honest. Use only facts and make sure they are accurate.
- Avoid educational jargon. Some education terminology may not be understood by people outside the educational community and may confuse the recipient.

Format of the letter:

- Make sure the reason for the correspondence comes through immediately. Begin with an opening statement that is strong and gets directly to the point.
- Create a continuing record.
  - Acknowledge the letter received from your correspondent and refer to its date and complaint.
  - Refresh your reader's memory about a sequence of events.
  - Thank the correspondent for expressing his or her concern.
- The body of the letter or e-mail should be direct and not wordy.
  - Set the record straight.
  - If applicable, clarify what action is being taken and why.
  - Explain the nature of the problem, what is being done about it, and what parents and students are expected to do.
  - Be tactful. Make sure your comments are judicious and courteously written. Do not agitate the reader.
- The summation should defuse the situation.
  - Display a sense of empathy. Avoid a letter that sounds form-like and bureaucratic.
  - Make the reader feel you have taken his or her feelings, wishes, and circumstances into account. Projecting an attitude of genuine concern and acceptance of ideas is important to the success of your response.
- Closing remarks
  - Be firm, but professional.
  - Close on a positive note, thanking the reader for his or her viewpoint.
  - Display a true sense of concern—and offer help.
  - Always sign with a handwritten signature.

It is not common to receive an emotional letter or e-mail from a parent. Keep the situation in perspective. You have more than 100 students and, hopefully, have received only one emotional letter this year. Most of your parents are satisfied with what you are doing. If the parent took the time to write to you, then the concern is very important to this parent and needs your full attention. Do not dismiss a parent's concern with a, "He doesn't know what he is talking about!" or "She is nuts!" Assume that every form of communication may continue on to the principal or School Board. So take a positive approach and use this opportunity to communicate better with this parent, establish a rapport, find mutual agreement on a solution. You will be glad you spent a little extra time responding to the difficult letter from the outset.

Experiencing a Lockdown or National Emergency

There may come a time in your career when you experience a lockdown of your school. Everyone in the school will be ordered to stay put until they receive further instructions from the principal or other authority figure. Sadly, a number of schools have faced lockdowns because some students or other individuals are bent on creating mayhem in the facility. Students have been killed and injured in such situations. The lockdown could be a consequence of some sort of national emergency, which affects the community at large. In either case, a lockdown can be a traumatic event.

As a teacher, you may be called on to play a critical role in protecting your students. You should be prepared for such an event. Every school should have an emergency plan in your Teacher Handbook. If you haven't been briefed on this, ask your department chairperson where and how you can familiarize yourself with the plan. The plan usually contains detailed instructions for the teacher to follow in a variety of scenarios. Examples of teacher duties are:

- Lock your classroom doors upon hearing a prearranged announcement.
- Take attendance and make sure all your students are accounted for. If a student has left the room but is believed to be in the school, call the office immediately to report the names of students unaccounted for.
- Keep students away from the windows.
- Don't allow students to leave the classroom until an all-clear message is received.
- Keep your students calm and quiet so directions over the loud speaker can be heard.

Many emergency plans do not address what you should say to the students. You are told to keep the students calm, but in such a situation, there are bound to be lots of questions and few answers in the beginning. The best thing you can do is assure students that they are safe. Go over the emergency plan with them and explain that the school administration is in communication with essential personnel. If there is a telephone in your classroom, explain that the phone lines must be left open so that you can receive or make any emergency phone calls. Be sure you are familiar with your school's policy on students' use of cell phones, particularly during emergencies.

If students feel the situation is under control, they will stay calm. If you are panicky and nervous, you may transfer those feelings to your students, and they may be more difficult to control. Keep your students occupied by telling some stories or discussing a topic that should capture their attention and take it off the boredom of waiting for word about the emergency.

During the events of September 11, 2001, a teacher had several students in her class whose fathers and mothers worked at the Pentagon. The teenagers were scared and confused. After what seemed like an eternity with little new information, and many distraught faces looking to her, the teacher began talking about fairy tales. She told the students that during medieval times, there was little hope of improving one's lot in life. Life was hard and short for the peasants. If a person was not a member of royalty, the only way he or she would ever live that kind of life was for magic to transform the person into a princess or a prince, or transform mundane objects into gold or jewels. She soon had the students so involved in the origin of fairy tales and why they were popular, that time went by and her students were able to make it through the class period without being traumatized by the events of that day. There was no manual for 9/11 and teachers did what they could with their students. Every teacher later told stories of how they got through that day and it all came down to being in control and staying calm.

Students look to you as their leader and will feel secure if they see that you have your wits about you. Be honest with your students and reassure them that there is a plan in place. Do not let them get carried away with the "what ifs?" Stick to the facts that are known at the time. If there is a TV on during a lockdown, news channel reports may be incorrect or incomplete. Some reports may sensationalize the events to the point that your students could become unglued, so check your school's emergency plan to see what it recommends in such a situation. Unfortunately, there are no perfect plans for extraordinary events like these. In the absence of clear guidance, go with your instincts and remember to make your students' safety and well-being your number one concern.

Am I ready for challenging moments?

☐ I have a back-up plan always ready in case my lesson is not going as planned.
- ☐ I have planned an extra activity for the end of my lesson in case there is time remaining.

☐ I have developed a strategy to deal with student confrontations and am prepared to defuse the situation.

☐ I am prepared for any technology malfunction.
- ☐ I have an extra bulb for my overhead projector on hand or I know where to find one.
- ☐ I have plenty of transparencies so that I can use the overhead projector in an emergency.
- ☐ I plan to post a copy of the presentation online or in the room.
- ☐ I plan to save all my work on a flash drive or school server.
- ☐ I have an extension cord in my desk in case a wall outlet is dead.
- ☐ I have plenty of batteries on hand.
- ☐ I have checked all laptops and/or computers and I know they have CD drives.
- ☐ I have also check to make sure all computers are working.
- ☐ I checked the light in the LCD projector and the cords connecting it to the computer.
- ☐ I've checked to make sure all computers in the lab have the software loaded and ready to be switched over to the target language.
- ☐ In case the server in my district or school crashes, I have an emergency lesson handy.
- ☐ I have a flash drive I can use in emergencies and will keep it with me at all times.
- ☐ I know where a second CD player is located in case the one in my classroom fails.
- ☐ I have extra CDs and cassette tapes in case a student needs one.

☐ I have a plan in case a parent shows up unexpectedly for a parent conference.

☐ I know exactly what to do in case of a lockdown.

☐ I know all the students in my classes that have a medical need or take prescription medication for a medical condition.

☐ I know how to modify a lesson or activity in case the class is interrupted and I do not have as much time remaining as I had planned.

☐ I am prepared to be able to communicate effectively with parents and answer difficult e-mails or letters.

Reflection

What aspect of this chapter worked well?

What would I change for next year?

How would I change it?

What additional resources do I need to gather for next year?

Chapter 4 The Years Ahead

The first year is drawing to a close and you have made it! It is a time to celebrate your accomplishments, but at the same time it is essential to reflect on this past year and develop a plan to refine your teaching strategies so that next year can be even better. Where should you begin? This chapter will guide your analysis of what worked, what needs more attention, and what resources are available to help you through the rest of your career. The skillful teacher is a life-long learner. It is important to change with your clientele and stay current on new practices. You'll find that what worked one year may not work the next. Be flexible and be prepared to research best practices, review what you created, revise what was not effective, refine what worked well, and keep an open mind regarding change.

Continual learning and review will keep your teaching career strong and enjoyable. Just like a surgeon, lawyer, or engineer, you must stay current with new research and developments. Ways to accomplish this include attending workshops, seminars, demonstrations; collaborating with colleagues on learning; and improvement programs. Embrace change; it energizes thinking. Prepare yourself each year to greet students with different strengths, varied abilities, diverse backgrounds, distinct needs, and a variety of learning styles. If you figure you can pull last year's lesson plans out of your files without refining them to meet the needs of this new group of individuals, you soon will be scratching your head wondering why something that worked marvelously last year is not working at all this year. If you assess each year in order to learn how to be better prepared for the next, not only will you develop a wealth of resources, but you will also sharpen your teaching techniques to meet the needs of the ever-changing student population in today's society.

Reflections

When you review your past year, take out your goals and objectives for that year. Did you meet your goals? Did you meet your objectives? What are your indicators? What evidence do you have? Analyze each aspect of the past year by quarter or marking period. Go through your grade book and plan book to see what notations you made along the way. Use the following questions to rate your performance:

Assessments:

- Did I have to retest because the majority of my students did not score as well as I had hoped on the previous assessment? List the assessments as a reminder.
- Did the assessments actually measure what I had taught? If not, list the ones that need revision.
- Did I vary the assessments to measure not only content information, but also interpersonal communication, presentational and interpretive abilities, cultural knowledge, and informal use of the language?
- How often did I assess? (The fewer grades you have, the heavier the weight each one has). Did my grades really measure what the students were able to do? Did I feel at any time that the quarter grade was off the mark?
- Were my assessments aligned with those of my colleagues? Did I collaborate with teachers who teach the same language and level that I do?

- Do I know if all students were given equal opportunities to speak in class? Did my class participation grade really measure this?

Lesson plans:

- Which lessons were my most successful ones? Why?
- Which lessons created confusion? Why?
- Which lessons took the most time to complete?
- Which lessons needed the least time to complete?
- Which theme or topic needs more emphasis based on the results seen on assessments?
- Do I need to pace myself better? Did I spend too much time on some topics and not enough on others?
- Is there a topic or language structure I did not cover?
- Did I have to speed up at the end of the year to get everything in?

Balance:

- Did I give my students enough opportunity to use the language? Did my assessments measure their progress in this area?
- Were my classes more teacher-directed or student-directed?
- Did I vary my instructional practices?
- Was enough time spent on having my students listen to native speakers of the language? Did I assess listening comprehension often enough?
- Am I satisfied with how many opportunities I gave my students to read authentic material? Did I teach my students to read?
- How often did I require my students to write?
- At the end of the year could my students write on their own without a "check list" of what they were to include in the writing sample?
- Did I teach my students the writing process or did I expect them to already know how to write?

Communication with students and parents:

- How often did parents call me saying they needed more clarification of my expectations?
- How often did students tell me they didn't know I was going to assess certain aspects of the chapter or thematic unit.
- How often did students not turn things in because they didn't know it was due?
- How often did students fail to make up missed work?
- How often did students come unprepared for the day's lesson?
- Did I miss any parent conferences or not return e-mails/phone calls?
- Did I fail to inform the parents of any students who dropped two letter grades before the end of the marking period?

Homework:

- Did my students complain that my homework assignments were merely "busy work?"
- Did my assignments give students the opportunity to practice what was taught during the class period?
- How frequently did students comment that they didn't understand the homework assignment? Which assignment?
- Did I ever use homework or grade homework as a punishment?

Classroom management:

- Did my students show me respect?
- Did I have to bribe my students to get them to do what I wanted?
- Did I issue ultimatums? If so, did I follow through on them?
- Was I consistent in implementing my classroom rules?
- Did the administration support me when I had a problem?
- Was I supported by a member of the department or a mentor teacher when I had a classroom management issue?
- How often did I have to tell my class to pay attention?
- Did I have the attention of all my students when I was teaching or did their attention often stray?
- Did the students understand and follow my classroom routines? If not, was it because I didn't have routines firmly established?

Staff development and training:

- Did I take advantage of staff development opportunities?
- How often did I collaborate with my colleagues?
- Did I ask questions or try to figure out things on my own?
- Did I seek help from my department chairperson or mentor?
- Did I read any professional journals or research during the year that helped me?
- Did use all the technology available to me?

After completing a self-assessment of your first year, the next step is developing a plan for next year. It's important to identify areas of need so you can devote time and study to them before the new school year begins. You will be amazed how much concentration you can give to the curriculum when you don't have school year distractions.

Revisions for Next Year

After identifying areas that need revision or refinement, it is important to prioritize your improvement goals. Every area mentioned in the preceding section has an impact on student achievement, but if you look at your answers in each section, is there an area that stands out above the others? If so, you will want to make this a priority area for improvement for the following year.

On the other hand, if you feel that your students achieved what you thought they should throughout the year, but you want to vary your assessments to include more speaking performance assessments next year, then you need to examine your answers in the Balance section above to see if you were giving students enough opportunity to perform during class time. Your priority list then, would show the following areas of focus:

1. Revise lesson plans to allow more time for partner activities to improve oral communication.
2. Give students an opportunity to use a rubric to rate themselves on a performance task in order to better understand expectations.
3. Develop two speaking performance assessments (one informal and one formal) per chapter.
4. Allow time for students to set goals and keep a portfolio to chart progress on performance assessments. This should include self-assessments.

Likewise, if classroom management is an area you have identified for improvement, then develop an improvement plan. The following suggestions are recommended:

- Participate in summer workshops that focus on classroom management strategies.
- Ask the administration if you can have release time during the last month of school to observe a teacher who is recognized for having good classroom management skills. (This is usually a time when students can be rather challenging. You will pick up excellent strategies during times full of distractions.)
- Ask a colleague to observe you during his or her planning period before the end of the school year. Sit down with this teacher and take note of what he or she has to say. Don't be defensive. Remember, it is hard to see what habits we have formed while we are teaching.
- Give your students an evaluation survey form at the end of the year. Students will usually take the time to express their opinions, indicating areas of satisfaction and frustrations with the course. Read between the lines and use this information to your benefit.

When you have gathered the data you need to make revisions, develop a plan and stick to it. If you discover that you need to be more consistent, only make rules you will be able to enforce with every student all the time. Go back over your class rules and see if they need modifications. If the administration failed to back you up on a certain rule, revise it to be consistent with school policy.

Be certain that you list the essential elements needing revisions for continued success. It is easy to get sidetracked and spend the whole summer redesigning your bulletin board when assessments should be your real focus. Don't be afraid to ask for advice. See if colleagues have helpful material they are willing to share. You do not want to reinvent the wheel.

Successful Solutions

Nobody can give you solutions to every problem, but there are resources out there to help you find them. I often hear new teachers say, "If only I had known he or she could have helped me. The information was there all along, but I didn't have time to look through all the ancillaries during the school year." Or "I can't believe I created all of this from scratch and later found out my colleague had something similar I could have used."

The following tips may lead you to some solutions you have been looking for:

- Find out early what your teaching assignment will be for next year and collaborate with a veteran teacher before the school year ends.
- Go through any ancillaries that are available with your textbook series. See if the publisher supplies a manual with lesson plan ideas and read chapters that focus on the areas that gave you the most difficulties.
- Read the teacher edition of your textbook. Look for any suggestions the publishers have written prior to each chapter.
- Check with curriculum specialists in the central office of your district about any workshops planned for fall of the next school year.

- Collaborate with teachers who have taught the level above the one you will be teaching next year so that you have a clear picture of where you want your students to be at the end of next year.
- Check the Internet for any educational research that might lead you to strategies that can assist in teaching certain topics and getting the best results out of your students.
- Go to your professional library and read educational journals that address your areas of concern.
- Get involved in summer curriculum projects. These projects often give you the opportunity to connect with teachers from other schools and exchange ideas. Even though you are a new teacher, there are projects that can use your input and creativity.
- Look for summer professional development opportunities.
- Check to see what course offerings are available at local colleges or universities.
- Look through the bookroom at your school to see if there are additional resources that may be tucked away from previous years.
- Ask teachers who have recently retired if they would be willing to donate their materials to your school.
- Check with your PTA president to see if funds are available to purchase materials that you have identified as necessary for your program.
- Check with the librarian to see if there are any funds to add reading material for students in the target language.
- Collaborate with teachers in other disciplines to see if they have materials you can use to enrich your curriculum.
- Check the elementary resources and see if there are any materials you can use for your beginning language classes. (Many posters and handouts used at that level can be very useful in your courses, although you may need to label the target language over the English).
- Visit teacher stores and be inventive about finding materials available in other subjects that can be used in a foreign language class.

Professional Organizations

It is understandable that the majority of your first year was spent keeping one step ahead of your students. You may not have realized how much help teachers can obtain at local, regional, and national conferences. In fact, most of these conferences offer a multitude of workshops on topics that can benefit all language educators. Vendors display a variety of supplemental materials that can aid classroom teachers. Publishers often have all the ancillaries on display and will demonstrate their usefulness. Sometimes vendors give out free samples of classroom materials and products that you can try out in your classroom. Of course, they come with order forms, catalogues, vendors' business cards, in the interest of keeping you in touch with them.

Another important aspect of conferences is the networking you can do with colleagues in your field. You often see teachers trading e-mail addresses and promising to send one another material. At conference workshops there is usually time at the end for questions and discussion. Often there are opportunities to have your questions answered by experts in the field and discuss them with colleagues from far and wide.

Most professional organizations offer members a wealth of services, such as publications, research data, professional development opportunities, scholarships, competitions, testing services, listservs, study abroad opportunities, advocacy committees, and much more. Nearly all organizations have websites. Conference information is readily available months in advance. Workshop descriptions can be downloaded prior to a conference so teachers can see what's being offered that might help them. Hotel and travel prices usually are discounted for conference attendees. If registration, hotel, travel, and meals come to more than your budget can afford, there may be sources of support. For example, many school districts will either pay for teachers' conference registration and/or for the substitute day teachers will need to attend the conference.

Teachers sometimes forget that a school's PTA has funds that can offset the cost of conferences. It may be a matter of submitting a proposal and a request for the entire amount and seeing what's available for you. Ask your school administration if funds are set aside for staff development. Be prepared to offer to do turn-around training upon your return. The cost of sending you to a conference can benefit the entire department. It is surprising that many teachers do not ask for assistance. But it will cost you nothing to apply for it and the pay-off can be just what you need. You will surely never get what you don't ask for.

Credit for attending a conference is also a real bonus. Check with your school system and make sure you understand what types of professional development are required for re-certification. Generally all conferences are approved for required points. Before attending a conference, find out what you will need to document your attendance. After attending a conference or two, you may want to submit a proposal to present a workshop on your own. If you have a lesson or materials that you find very successful, you certainly want to share your strategies with your colleagues!

Overseas Travel/Educational Trips

A student trip to your target language country can be a marvelous experience for you and your students. You can imagine the value of using what you have learned in the classroom with peers who are natives of the country. On such a trip even students who have practiced the language and learned about the culture for several years exclaim, "The houses really do look like this!" as the tour bus weaves through the countryside. Students do not think you made it all up—but the foreign culture and language do not become a reality until they are there looking at everything that was just a picture in a book prior to the trip.

One of a language teacher's greatest joys is to watch students interact with local residents, shopkeepers, bus drivers, and manage on their own the language skills you taught them. Most of these educational travel opportunities are package tours with guides who remain with the group for the entire trip. Travel is prearranged and includes sightseeing excursions with local guides who tell the history of the places you visit. These tours usually included hotel accommodations, transportation, museum and historic site entrance tickets, guides and most meals. Trips like these can take a year to plan in cooperation with parents and other supporters.

With an enterprise this ambitious, there are caveats you'll want to heed before you agree to take students overseas:

- Have an experienced teacher travel with you to help shepherd your students. Make sure he or she has traveled abroad with students before.
- Have one adult for every five or six students and assign each adult responsibility for the same students for the entire trip.
- Have a photocopy of every student's passport before you depart and throughout the trip.
- Have passport checks three or four times a day. Just ask students to hold their passport up so you can see them every time you are about to pull away in the bus.
- Never allow students to drink alcohol in a foreign country away from their parents, even if you have the parent's permission. Everyone reacts to alcohol differently and an adverse reaction could have you taking a student to a foreign hospital or bailing one out of a foreign jail and leaving you facing a lawsuit. Many teachers have expressed regret at allowing students to have "just one" glass of beer or wine at dinner. It is not worth a lawsuit just to have a minor "experience" the culture to this degree in another country.
- Make sure students and parents understand the rules before departing. Do not hesitate to send a student home if he or she endangers himself or the group.
- Encourage students to have a budget so that they know exactly how much they can spend each day on souvenirs.
- Use a tour company that is well-established and has insurance that will cover cancellation, illness, lost luggage, and travel interruptions.
- Make sure you read every line of the contract, explain everything precisely to parents, and have an enormous amount of personal liability insurance coverage.

Trips like these can be very rewarding if planned and organized correctly. Bumps in the road can come with misunderstanding the contract (e.g., what is covered, what isn't covered, handling tipping, and the like). Students will remember the experience for a long time to come. Your first experience taking students abroad will also be rewarding if you prepare for the unknown well in advance.

Exchange programs are another means of overseas travel for students. Students usually stay in a host family's home for three weeks to a year, depending on the program. These experiences give students true insight into the people, the culture, and the language of a country. Not only are these students able to fine-tune their language ability, they also have experiences that could never be replicated in a classroom. Generally the students from the host county will come to the United States to stay with your students for a similar period of time. Bonds created in these programs can last a lifetime.

Am I prepared for another successful year?

☐ I have answered the questions regarding the past year in this chapter.

☐ After answering the questions, I know what I want to do differently next year and what I want to keep the same.

☐ I plan to join a professional organization.

☐ I plan to attend conferences and be a presenter.

☐ I plan to seek some type of leadership role within the school community.

☐ I plan to research opportunities for my students to get additional exposure to native speakers of the target language.

Reflection

What aspect of this year was successful?

What is the first thing I plan to revise or refine for next year?

How should I revise it?

What outside resources do I have available to me to accomplish this?

How do I plan to get more involved on a local, regional, or national level?

Appendix

Characteristics of Effective Foreign Language Instruction*

The National Association of District Supervisors of Foreign Languages has identified the following characteristics of effective foreign language instruction. These guidelines provide a basis for common understanding and communication among evaluators, observers, and practitioners in classrooms where foreign/second languages are taught. The Characteristics focus on the students who are the recipients of effective foreign language instruction.

The Characteristics reflect the National Standards for Foreign Language Learning (1996) and focus on the five goal areas of Communication, Connections, Comparisons, Cultures, and Communities. The Characteristics reflect also the importance of language learning strategies, diverse learning styles, the use of authentic cultural documents, and the use of technology as an instructional tool. The Characteristics are a companion resource to the National Standards for Foreign Language Learning, state frameworks, and local curriculum guides.

1. The teacher sets high expectations for all students, designs assessment, and organizes instruction to engage and motivate all learners.
2. The teacher and students communicate purposefully in the target language as listeners, speakers, readers, writers, and viewers.
3. There is more student activity than teacher activity in most lessons. Student activity includes student to student interactions as well as teacher to student interactions. Students work independently, in pairs, and in groups. Students ask and answer questions and they create with language.
4. Students take risks as language learners because the learning environment is positive and supportive.
5. When error correction is appropriate, students are given opportunities, including wait-time, to self-correct. Teacher correction of student errors is often done through follow-up review and reteaching strategies.
6. Assessments are ongoing. Students are assessed formally and informally on how well they are able to meet the objectives of the lesson. Continuous self-assessments for students and teachers are encouraged.
7. Students use language specific learning strategies and are encouraged to assess their own progress.
8. Culture is a natural component of language use in all activities.
9. All students are guided to use all levels of thinking skills, e.g., they repeat, recognize, and recall as well as apply, create, and predict.
10. The diverse learning styles of all students are considered in the teacher's instructional planning.
11. Students have positive attitudes toward cultural diversity which are often demonstrated in the learning environment.
12. The physical environment including displays of student work is instructional, motivational, and informative.
13. Students and teachers are not text-bound during instructional time. It is obvious that the text is a tool, not the curriculum.
14. Students and teachers use a variety of print and non-print materials including authentic target language sources.
15. Technology, as appropriate and available, is used by students and teachers to facilitate learning and teaching.

NOTE: Listening, speaking, and authentic non-print materials are emphasized, but to a lesser degree, in Latin and Classical Greek instruction.

*Revised and Approved at Annual Meeting, November 1999

The Characteristics of Effective Foreign Language Instruction were developed in collaboration with and based on work done by the Montgomery County Maryland Public Schools.

Afterword

When you ask first-year language teachers why they chose education, the response usually goes something like this: "I wanted to make a difference in the lives of kids and instill in them a love of language learning." Similarly, when you attend a retirement reception to honor an educator who has devoted his or her life to education, retirees often reflect on events associated with specific students who made their entire careers worthwhile. One can conclude, then, that educators never lose the desire to be a positive force in our students' lives. The drive to make an impact on the lives of others constitutes the bedrock of why we become involved in education in the first place. Those who have successful careers in the field keep their focus and are able to reflect on the difference they have made in the lives of students and colleagues. For some novice teachers, however, the ideal becomes clouded by the day-to-day demands and pressures of teaching.

It is a well-documented fact that many teachers entering the profession leave within the first few years and never return. Why is that? Is having the desire to influence the lives of students not enough? What role can veterans play in helping to keep others in the profession? We are all familiar with stories of teachers who start their careers with boundless energy and creative ideas and quickly become disillusioned with duties and responsibilities that seemingly have little or nothing to do with classroom instruction and individual students. The reasons most often given for leaving the profession are also known. Some cite a lack of support from their peers and administrators, while others are overwhelmed by the workload. Still others say their background and training did not adequately prepare them for the demands of being a classroom teacher. Language teachers are also often disappointed that not all their students are passionate about learning another language and culture. Still others comment on perceived student apathy and misbehavior. The list goes on and on and should serve as a call to action to those of us who are devoting our lives to this profession.

What can we do to assist those who are newest to teaching? One thing career language educators must do is to discover how to support and to mentor new teachers more effectively. Just as the most effective teachers are reflective practitioners who constantly strive to improve their practice, veteran educators must become reflective in filling the needs of our profession as a whole. Many of us who have "made it" past those critical first few years can point to one or two colleagues who took us under their wing and helped us deal with the seemingly endless issues we faced during that first year in the classroom. For example, during my first year of teaching, a special colleague spent countless hours helping me to plan lessons, troubleshooting problems with a test I spent hours developing, and giving me a heads up about important deadlines throughout the year. At the same time, this colleague implemented a number of activity ideas I suggested, which made me feel like I was giving something back to her for all the time she spent helping me. Mentoring means more than showing the new teacher where the photocopier is and how to use the electronic gradebook—it means developing a mutually beneficial ongoing professional relationship. The novice teacher can energize the veteran teacher with new ideas, while the veteran teacher is there to help anticipate roadblocks and to listen critically to the highs and lows in order to encourage the new educator to think critically about their lessons and interactions with students.

Another thing current language teachers must do is to recruit their students to become language teachers. Some students will be attracted to our profession if they recognize and sense the enthusiasm and passion we have for teaching languages. Students size up their teachers quickly and know which ones genuinely enjoy what they do. Given the critical need for language teachers, however, we may need to more directly point out to students the reasons to become a language teacher. Talk to your students about why you became a teacher and what you like most about it. Encourage students to practice teaching the language they are learning with friends, family, and others. Explain the travel benefits and ongoing life-long learning opportunities associated with being a teacher. Sharing this information with others will not only serve to recruit people to the profession, but it will also hopefully remind you of why you became a teacher in the first place and the support mechanisms that are in place to help you stay focused on "making a difference in the lives of students."

Everyone needs to feel supported and appreciated for what we do—it serves to give us positive reinforcement about the job we are doing and helps us retain focus on the best aspects of the education business. The intent of this book is to provide another layer of support for beginning teachers by helping them to anticipate what to expect during the first year of teaching and beyond. It can certainly be helpful to any first year teachers who read it but, in my opinion, the power of the publication lies in its potential to serve as a mentoring tool. Use the ideas and questions posed throughout the work to begin discussions with new teachers at your school or district. Empower your new colleagues by talking through parent conferences and rehearsing Back-to-School Night presentations. Assist them in making the templates provided applicable for your school/district. Finally, any teacher can benefit from reflecting on the end of year questions provided, so use them to strengthen your practice as well as the practice of your colleagues. By collaborating as a team of language professionals, we should be able to better mentor our newest colleagues and retain them for years to come!

For more information about mentoring, go to www.actfl.org.

David Jahner, Foreign Language Director
Gwinnett County (GA) Public Schools

The author would like to express thanks to the following people and organizations who contributed to this guide:

Fairfax County Public Schools (VA)

Georgia Department of Education

National Association of District Supervisors of Foreign Languages (NADSFL)

Consortium for Assessing Performance Standards: A New Jersey FLAP Grant Project
Project Directors:
Jacqueline Gilbert, West Orange Public Schools
Mary Mackenzie, East Brunswick Public Schools
Martin Smith & Beatrice Yetman, Edison Public Schools
Carol Meulener & Rosanne Zeppieri, West Windsor-Plainsboro Public Schools

Ruth D. Chang

Lucrecia Chivukula

Susan Crooks

Greg Duncan

Yu He

David Jahner

Mimi Met

Laura Terrill

Please consult the Publications section of the ACTFL website (www.actfl.org) for information about:

Standards for Foreign Language Learning in the 21st Century

ACTFL Performance Guidelines for K–12 Learners

Integrated Performance Assessment (IPA) Manual

All appendixes from this handbook can be downloaded from the Members section of the ACTFL website (www.actfl.org).